GRAFT

HOME. STORY.

GRAFT
HOME. STORY.

NEW RESIDENTIAL AND HOSPITALITY ARCHITECTURE

WITH A FOREWORD BY DANIEL LIBESKIND
BIRKHÄUSER BASEL

CONTENTS

8 FOREWORD
DANIEL LIBESKIND

10 PARAGON APARTMENTS
BERLIN | GERMANY

22 CBD BEIJING
BEIJING | CHINA

26 HOLISTIC LIVING
BERLIN | GERMANY

36 ECKWERK
BERLIN | GERMANY

44 BIRDS ISLAND
KUALA LUMPUR | MALAYSIA

52 VILLA VIENNA
VIENNA | AUSTRIA

60 PITT STUDIO
LOS FELIZ | USA

66 TOR149
BERLIN | GERMANY

76 PANORAMA TOWERS
LAS VEGAS | USA

80 TEMPLINER STRASSE
BERLIN | GERMANY

86 LOFT HAUSVOGTEIPLATZ
BERLIN | GERMANY

96 VILLA M
BERLIN | GERMANY

100 LAKESIDE VILLA BERLIN
BERLIN | GERMANY

108 WAVE
BERLIN | GERMANY

114 ALMSTADTSTRASSE
BERLIN | GERMANY

122 LOFT HAMBURG
HAMBURG | GERMANY

130 VILLA J
SOUTHERN ENGLAND
UNITED KINGDOM

136
LOFT GLEIMSTRASSE
BERLIN | GERMANY

146
HEIMAT2
BERLIN | GERMANY

152
MAKE IT RIGHT
NEW ORLEANS | USA

160
NAMIBIA AFFORDABLE HOUSING
THREE SITES | NAMIBIA

168
TELTOWN
TELTOW | GERMANY

172
BRICKS
BERLIN | GERMANY

182
CHARLIE LIVING
BERLIN | GERMANY

188
BLÜTENVIERTEL
CAPUTH | GERMANY

192
AUENFLÜGEL
BERLIN | GERMANY

200
HAUS KOCH
BERLIN | GERMANY

206
AO PROJECT
TOKYO | JAPAN

214
BEIJING CHATEAU
BEIJING | CHINA

218
FUXIN MIXED USE
BEIJING | CHINA

222
MOONRAKER
BURBANK | USA

226
CAELA LIGHTING SYSTEM

228
FSB 1246

230
FAT TONY

232
DRIFT INTERPROFIL

234
KANERA SINK

238
PHANTOM TABLE

240
BIBLIOLONGUE

242
RESIDENTIAL PROJECTS
WORLDWIDE

248
NEW WAYS OF DWELLING
THEORY

276
OLD MILL HOTEL
BELGRADE | SERBIA

288
HOTEL GAMMARTH
TUNIS | TUNISIA

300
FAMILY HOUSE SANKT AUGUSTIN
ST. AUGUSTIN | GERMANY

308
HOTEL AND SPA SEEZEITLODGE
BOSTALSEE | GERMANY

316
BRLO BRWHOUSE
BERLIN | GERMANY

322
YOUTH HOSTEL MUNICH
MUNICH | GERMANY

330
HOTEL IVERIA
TBILISI | GEORGIA

344
W HOTEL
NEW YORK | USA

350
VERTICAL VILLAGE
DUBAI | U.A.E.

356
CITY CENTER'S ARIA
LAS VEGAS | USA

364
HOTEL Q!
BERLIN | GERMANY

374
HOTEL LOFER
LOFER | AUSTRIA

384
THE EMPEROR
BEIJING | CHINA

396
SAMANA LUXURY RESORT
SAMANA | DOMINICAN REPUBLIC

400
STACK RESTAURANT & BAR
LAS VEGAS | USA

406
DESERT CANYON RESORT
DUBAI | U.A.E.

412
FIX RESTAURANT
LAS VEGAS | USA

418
DALIAN AMBER BAY BEACH
DALIAN | CHINA

424
GINGKO BACCHUS
CHENGDU | CHINA

436
BRAND RESTAURANT
LAS VEGAS | USA

442
CHANGBAISHAN SKI JUMPS
WANGTIANE | CHINA

452
GALLERY HOTEL
BEIJING | CHINA

458
MYSTERY BAY
HAINAN | CHINA

468
W HOTEL AND RESORT
PALM SPRINGS | USA

474
WOK-A-LICIOUS
BERLIN | GERMANY

480
WATER CAY
TURKS AND CAICOS ISLANDS

492
BONDS CAY ISLAND
BAHAMAS

500
HOSPITALITY PROJECTS
WORLDWIDE

504
GRAFT WORLD

506
ABOUT GRAFT

508
GRAFTIES

FOREWORD

———

In a world dominated by architecture produced by "remote control", the work of GRAFT architects, founded by Lars Krückeberg, Wolfram Putz and Thomas Willemeit, reflects the opposite; work done with human compassion, human intelligence and the human soul. Architecture is a language that can be guided by history, storytelling and humanity. It is also a public art, framed by a civic context; it is about the culture of a place, and stories that have never been told.

This book of hotels and residential projects, built across the globe, deals with investigations into hospitality and explorations into its architectural expression. In the 21st century, the domestic environment is no longer to be seen as some mechanical, functionalistic machine, but it now relates to global memory. GRAFT uses architecture as a dynamic way forward and as an exploration of creativity, rather than creating finished products. Their designs for hybrid and highly flexible living spaces give context for an expression of pluralism and openness.

I have known GRAFT for years and have followed their architectural output continuously. I am particularly close to one of their partners, Thomas Willemeit, who used to work with me in our Berlin studio. GRAFT's commitment to architecture has been to elevate design to an elegant and hugely creative level. The content of this book offers an impressive array of hospitality works, both interior and exterior. They "test" the possibilities of architecture and bring it to a new and exciting realm.

Daniel Libeskind

———

PROJECT | Multi-family house

PARAGON APARTMENTS
BERLIN | GERMANY

The Paragon Apartments lie northeast of the intersection of Prenzlauer Allee and Danziger Strasse, between the dense block developments at Kollwitzplatz and Helmholzplatz and the open residential district bordering to the east. The new quarters, with 217 premium rental apartments, a kindergarten, a café and an organic supermarket, mediates between the urban qualities of the Prenzlauer Berg district and the adjacent park-like surroundings. Paragon augments the block without closing it entirely and presents a unique hybrid of perimeter block and open building. The development, comprising one renovated building and two newly constructed buildings, offers a solution to the need for diversity in a modern and urban housing project.

The starting point for the Paragon Apartments is a former hospital building located between Danziger Strasse and Fröbelplatz, that was built as a school in 1912. Its roof was dismantled and replaced with two new upper floors. Three other existing buildings, built at a later date, have been incorporated in the project and modified in size. Two new structures augment the existing buildings: one along Danziger Strasse and the other at the rear facing the Fröbelplatz. Together they connect to the perimeter block structure of the neighborhood.

The ensemble of Paragon Apartments has a total of three communal courtyards. A public space at the intersection creates an entrance situation that leads into the first inner

....

Left | Main entrance and hallway
Right | Community space and library

courtyard, from which all apartments can be reached. The main entrance of the old hospital still exists and is reached from the first courtyard. The old hallways and existing staircases to the upper floors are likewise integrated into the new design. The high ceilings of the old building give the apartments a spacious quality, as does the addition of new balconies.

The first courtyard can also be reached via an entrance from the Fröbelplatz, creating a partly private, partly public connection within the quarter – leading from the urban front to the calm green of the park at the rear. A community space that serves as a club room and includes a library for the tenants is situated on this path.

GRAFT developed an efficient housing cube for the project: a 2-room apartment cube with a size of 37.5 m² that forms a repeating module. Living and sleeping areas can be joined or divided by a sliding door. The bathroom, accessible from the hall and bedroom, joins the two as a passage. Fixed fittings within the cube are configured to maximise space in the apartment's living and sleeping areas, giving the space a loft-like character despite its small size.

Right top | View from the courtyard
Left bottom | Maisonette apartment in new construction
Right bottom | Balcony overlooking Danziger Strasse

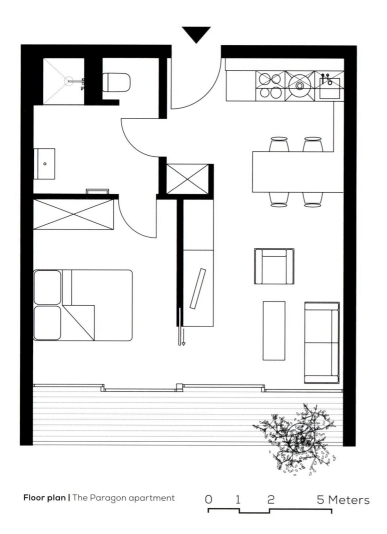

Floor plan | The Paragon apartment

Left | Main entrance
Right | Two-room apartment of 70m²

The apartments in the new building on Danziger Strasse have balconies of varying depth. Arranged next to and above one another in a shifting stacked pattern, they lend the façade an animated three-dimensional quality. Made of high-precision, light-colored prefabricated concrete elements, with generous glazed surfaces, the projecting edges of the cubes serve as solar shades.

The flexible concept of the cubes allows them to be combined to create larger apartments – up to 250m² – for the replacement roof structure on the old building. As such, the basic modular element of the new building – its DNA so to speak – appears to emerge from the structure on the Danziger Strasse and continue on over the rooftops towards the Fröbelplatz, integrating the old and new buildings into an ensemble. Although the new structures of the ensemble offer diverse living spaces, the appearance of the façade remains homogenous.

The perimeter block has not been closed entirely, allowing the historical urban structure of the old building to remain visible and leaving the green courtyards open to their surroundings. In the heart of one of the densest areas of Berlin, the new Paragon Apartments provide a large number of apartments with green surroundings and views overlooking the park and courtyards.

The ensemble's three communal courtyards are green areas with seating, and include a playground for children and parking spaces for bicycles. A café and a kindergarten adjoin the first courtyard, and the third courtyard features a private garden that leads on to the neighboring public park.

Site plan

0 5 10 20 Meters

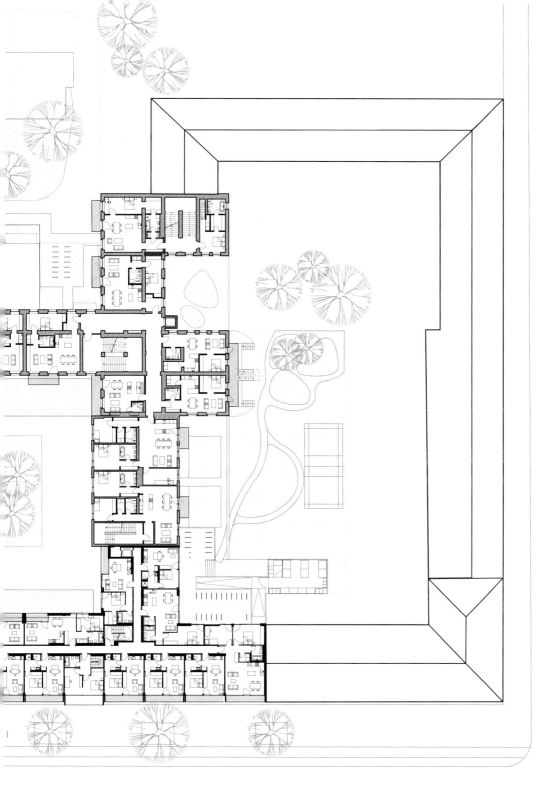

CLIENT | Trockland
YEAR | 2016
SIZE | 23,500m²
STATUS | Built

PROJECT | Masterplanning residential and business disctrict

CBD BEIJING
BEIJING | CHINA

GRAFT's proposal for the east extension of Beijing's business district envisages connecting all land parcels to follow the flow of pedestrians. In the center of the district is a central park, partially raised above ground providing space for public, commercial and entertainment facilities beneath it. Large openings in the park allow daylight and fresh air to penetrate to the levels below.

The uppermost indoor level is a railway station with retail areas around it, while lower levels contain underground parking. The surrounding towers are articulated by carving plazas out of the podium levels and elevating the towers above ground. Bridges connect the park level to the surrounding areas and residents can choose to walk above ground through the park to their offices or to walk indoors through the shopping spaces.

The new railway station connects residential areas to the CBD and its retail facilities and green spaces, reducing dependency on private cars and taxis and making street life more vibrant as a result.

CLIENT | SOHO China
YEAR | 2010
SIZE | 300,000m²
STATUS | In progress

PROJECT | Plus-energy houses with e-mobility concept

HOLISTIC LIVING
BERLIN | GERMANY

GRAFT's design for a single-family house and two semi-detached houses combines the aspects of mobility, energy and healthy living with environmentally-friendly construction. The project's holistic approach encompasses modern architecture, innovative building services and e-mobility as well as sustainability and physical health. The houses even generate a energy surplus that will be used to charge an e-car that the tenant rents with the house.

Every aspect of these intelligent homes is environmentally sustainable, from their design to their construction and operation. The building materials have been selected for sustainability across their entire life cycle and are natural and recyclable: the ceilings, walls and roof are made of wood and earth. These natural materials contribute to a healthy, pleasant indoor atmosphere and are paired with state-of-the-art technology that assures comfortable but environmentally-friendly living. Each building is triple-glazed and thermally-insulated, including the cellars, to prevent thermal bridges.

The buildings have a combination of underfloor heating system and mechanical ventilation with a highly-efficient heat recovery system that the residents can control. Some of the electricity is generated by photovoltaic cells on the roof.

....

Left | Single-family house

This spread | Living room

....

The total energy consumption of the house is less than that harvested from the PV elements. Any surplus of energy can be used to charge an e-car that the tenant rents together with the house. As such, the houses combine the aspects of mobility, energy and health to create a holistic and responsible future living experience.

Through their use of renewable energy, the three building units fulfil the requirements of the Plus-Energy House quality standard as set out by the German Federal Ministry of Transport, Building and Urban Affairs. The implementation planning was done by the international engineering firm BuroHappold Engineering. Aside from the use of innovative technology, healthy and eco-friendly materials and responsible construction methods, the design of the houses is to the highest architectural standards: smart floorplans locate private areas with panoramic views on the upper floors and large open communal areas on the ground floor. Indoor and outdoor spaces are connected by these shared living spaces. This role model for future living was completed in spring 2015.

———

This spread | Sections and floor plans single-family house

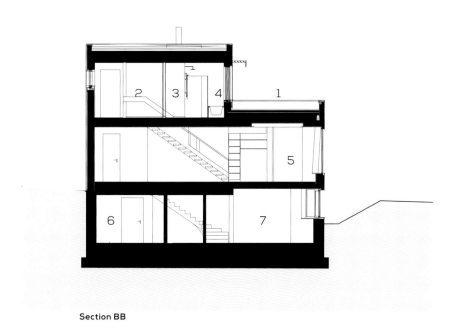

Section BB

1. Solar plant
2. Hallway
3. Lavatory
4. Bathroom
5. Dining Room
6. Installations, storage room
7. Lavatory

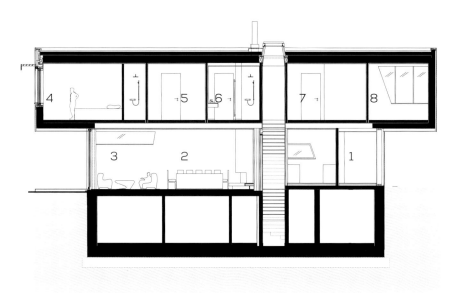

Section AA

1. Entrance
2. Dining room
3. Living room
4. Master bedroom
5. Room 1
6. Bathroom
7. Room 2
8. Room 3

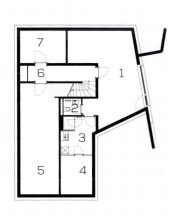

Basement

1. Hobby room
2. Lavatory
3. Bathroom
4. Storage room
5. Storage room, plant room
6. Hallway
7. Boiler room

Ground floor

1. Entrance
2. Dining room
3. Living room
4. Kitchen
5. Storage room
6. Lavatory
7. Terrace

1st floor

1. Master bedroom
2. Room 1
3. Bathroom
4. Room 2
5. Room 3

CONNECTIVITY OF INSIDE AND OUTSIDE

- Integration of indoor and outdoor spaces
- Integration of the buildings into the landscape
- Maximum level of transparency between garden and living room

HEALTHY MATERIALS

- Application of natural, ecological and local materials
- Avoidance of harmful emissions
- Recyclability of materials
- Reduction of waste through production, use, maintenance and demolition of used materials
- Healthy indoor climate

WATER MANAGEMENT

- Grey-water recovery unit for the garden
- Installation of a rainwater cistern

PLUS-ENERGY HOUSE

- Reduction of energy and resource consumption through efficient building equipment and appliances
- Provision of more primary as well as final energy than what will be required for usage
- Usage of regenerative energies (solar and geothermal energy)
- Reduction of the heat losses through controlled ventilator
- Energy management system to reduce the daily peak loads
- Installation of energy-efficient household appliances and lighting as well as mountings with low water consumptions

COMFORT AND WELL BEING

- Generous room layout
- Extensive views
- High living quality in community spaces
- Calm areas of retreat and privacy
- Heating of the rooms via floor heating and in the bathroom through additional towel radiators
- Bus system allows an increase of energy efficiency through building automation

MOBILITY WITHOUT CARBON DIOXIDE

- Carbon dioxide-neutral operation of one EV per house or semi-detached house through energy surplus of the houses
- Connection between mobility (EV) and immobility (architecture)

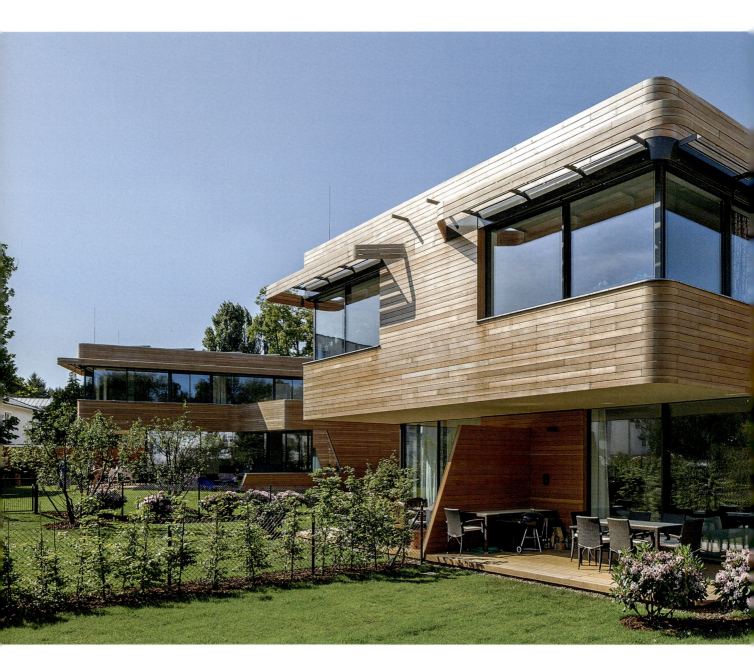

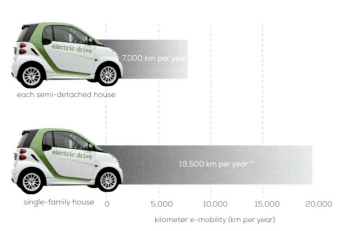

*Supposition: Maximum consumption e-Smart 20 kWh per 100km and average energy consumption

Surplus energy for electric mobility

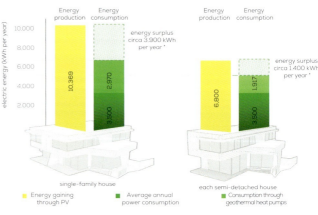

Energy required and energy pain (kWh per year)

CLIENT | Private Client
YEAR | 2014
SIZE | 1 x 707m² und 2 x 500m²
STATUS | Built

PROJECT | Affordable housing, high rise, student housing, mixed use

ECKWERK
BERLIN | GERMANY

Under the framework of open dialogue, the two architecture firms GRAFT and Kleihues + Kleihues, as well as the "Genossenschaft für urbane Kreativität" ("Cooperative for Urban Creativity") developed an exemplary complex of buildings which seeks to find answers to the social, economic and ecological questions of our times.

The central idea is to create an inspiring and vivid place which sets new benchmarks with respect to the relationship between work and living as well as between public life and privacy. Construction started in 2015 on the northern part of the "Holzmarkt" area along the River Spree which was home to the legendary "Bar 25" until 2011. The design for Eckwerk draws on the characteristic qualities of the location, picking up the grain of the surrounding streets and referring to the "Stadtbahnviadukt" which runs like a golden thread through the center of the city and is a defining element of the site. To the north, the complex steps up vertically in topographic steps, creating a passage between the building and the viaduct – a place of interaction with the main entrances and access to public functions. The solid base of the building complex is the same height as the viaduct, its roof acting as an urban

....

This spread | Public market space

terrace with a view out over the water. Placed on top of the plinth are five independently accessible towers, each providing highly flexible spaces which can be used either for working or living.

The terraced landscape of the interior space is designed as a multi-level public market place and serves as a hybrid indoor-outdoor area for the co-working spaces. Covered by a delicate steel and glass construction, it can be used all year round.

The decision to divide the program into separate towers is not only an attempt to meet the requirements of zoning laws but also creates a sense of openness as well as diverse views and outlooks, breaking down the boundary between the house and the city (private and public). The towers have a staggered arrangement decreasing in scale towards the river to afford direct views of the Spree, also from the buildings in the back row.

The five towers are connected by a publicly accessible "experience trail", the so-called "mountain path". It connects the separate parts of the ensemble and opens into semi-public spaces for interaction and relaxation. Meandering through the building, it can be accessed by the public without interfering with private work or living areas. It is conceived as a continuation of the Spree riverbank walk, as stipulated in the citizen-initiated referendum "Spree riverbank for all". By opening the site and much of the building to the public, it interweaves public circulation into a private development. In contrast to the solid, durable nature of the base of the complex, the towers embody lightness and changeability through their wooden frontage. Wood is both a renewable material and also part of the tradition of the site, the former riverside timber market.

The floor plans as well as the façades follow a modular design principle, making it possible to individually modify and adapt the building. Like urban acupuncture, the Eckwerk project manipulates the natural tendencies of socio-economic change in the urban matrix, proving that affordable housing in high price areas is possible.

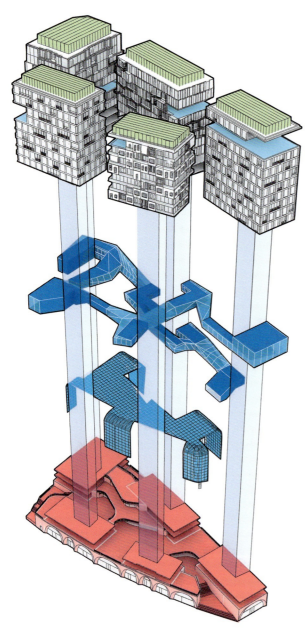

Explosion diagram

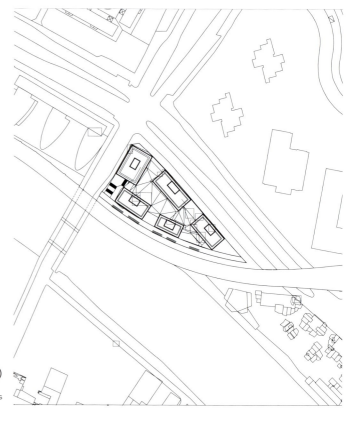

Site plan

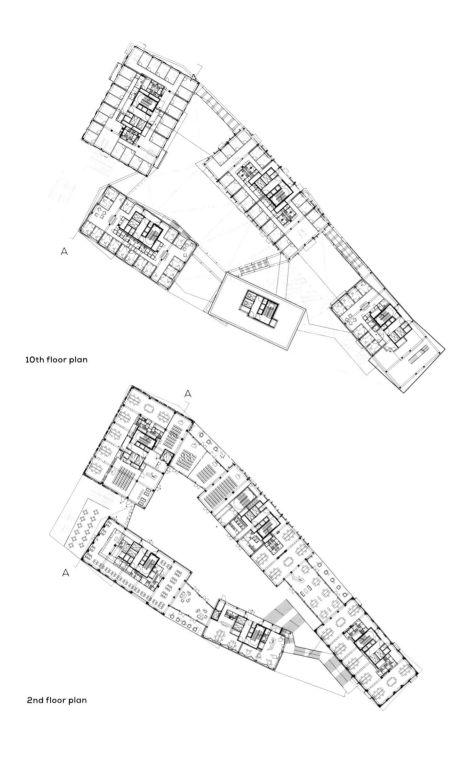

10th floor plan

2nd floor plan

CLIENT | Eckwerk, GuK cooperative (Genossenschaft für urbane Kreativität)
WORKGROUP | GRAFT with Kleihues + Kleihues
YEAR | 2016
SIZE | 34,000m²
STATUS | Under construction

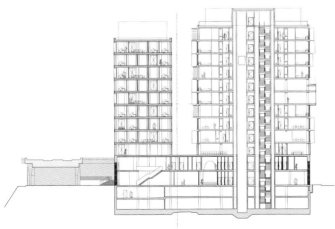

Section AA

PROJECT | Zero-energy villas, first prize invited design competition

BIRDS ISLAND
KUALA LUMPUR | MALAYSIA

The design for zero-energy villas in Kuala Lumpur explores territories of design that have emerged in response to a new, rising awareness of sustainable design, translating energy-saving requirements into poetic design solutions that are not only environmentally friendly and efficient, but also offer a new interpretation of the spaces we live in. The design presents a cost-saving response to warm climate habitation.

The living quarters have an expansive shaded outdoor living deck, while the primary living space is located in the cooler interior core. The silicon glass skin envelope serves as a multifunctional translucent shell, casting subtle shadows and creating changing patterns of view, while freeing the space from the bonds of traditional walls. Curtains can be drawn to enclose living spaces, creating privacy.

This strategy is geared to cutting waste and eliminating redundant energy systems. The optimized building skin doubles as a frame with integral rainwater and solar heat collection systems, acting as wind flow conductor, and distributing rainwater. The entire structure is set on piers, minimizing erosion and affording natural cooling by allowing air to flow unobstructed under the floor. Solar lotuses in the water nearby act as satellite energy collectors, providing the remainder of the energy needed for the structure to operate as a zero-energy building.

....

This spread | Perspective view of the North villa with the South villa in the background

Left | Interior
Right | Exploded perspective

....

The design concept for the zero-energy houses employs a holistic strategy that pairs the economic and environmental advantages of environmentally friendly living with the needs of a demanding, cosmopolitan clientele. Ecological and economical concerns should be perceived as augmenting rather than restricting modern lifestyles, improving living comfort while impacting less on the environment. An expansive outdoor living deck spans the width of the site, while the primary living space is contained within the cooler interior. A dynamic tensile structure encloses the interior space, maximizing the use and energy-efficiency of the space within. The thin building envelope creates a new relationship between indoors and outdoors.

The other living areas are arranged separately from each other, separated by channels of landscaped local vegetation. The fabric of the tensile skin flows over the interior, shaping and imbuing the spaces with subtle shadows and patterns, and providing glimpses of the outdoors. Heavy sliding curtains can be used to separate off private areas.

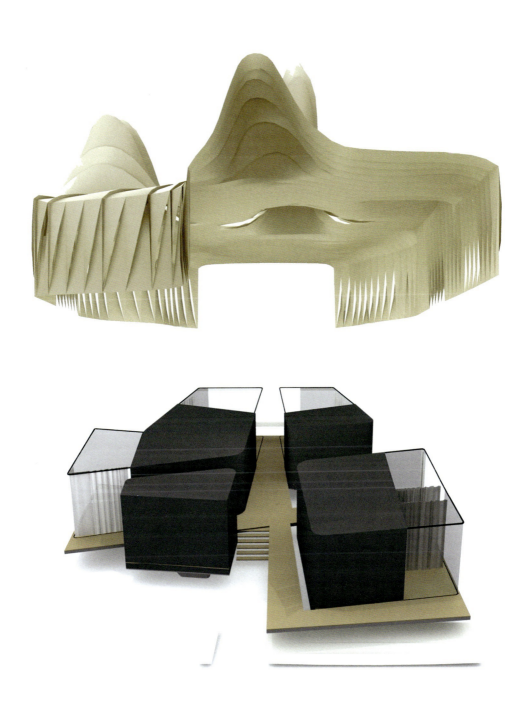

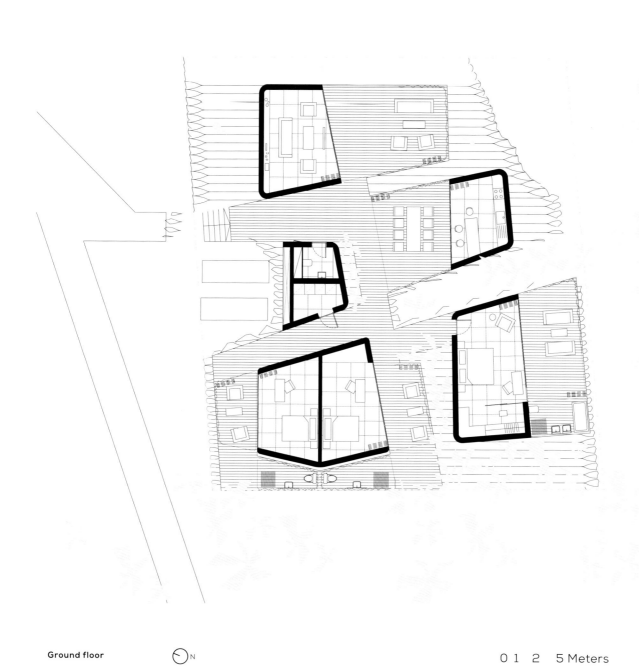

Ground floor

0 1 2 5 Meters

CLIENT | YTL Land Development
YEAR | 2007
SIZE | 1,100m²/villa
STATUS | In progress

PROJECT | Interior design, refurbishment

VILLA VIENNA
VIENNA | AUSTRIA

GRAFT was commissioned to redesign a former presidential villa in Vienna for a private art collector. The design focuses on adapting the villa to incorporate the art collection using new motifs and materials. Selected artworks as well as existing patterns are transferred into a new formal code with the help of the phenomena of reflecting surfaces. This new spatial concept creates an interplay between the traditional elements, the artworks and new spatial elements.

The design transforms the classical floor plan of the villa with its separate rooms and functions – vestibule, salon and loggia – into a continuous flowing space, weaving an architectural promenade through them linked scenographically by the works of art. Sliding doors ensure that all areas can still be used separately. The lobby, living room and gallery walk around an old staircase are recast in white and sandstone, and the stairs extended to lead to the library. The different historical themes are woven together by the idea of an exhibition. The gallery walk is mirrored on both sides and provided with a luminous ceiling, multiplying the objets d'art to a polychromatic effect.

The motif of reflection recurs in the bathroom where a Venetian mirror allows guests to glimpse into the lobby without being seen, creating a voyeuristic effect in reverse. Mirrors also connect the living room with the former loggia, drawing light deeper into the room.

....

Right | Kitchen with adjacent living room

This spread | Living room

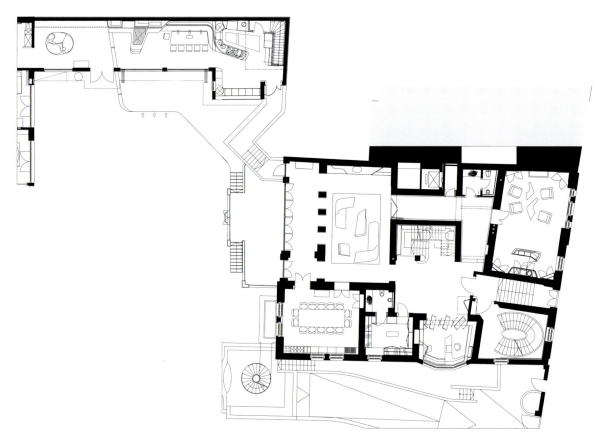

Floor plan

....

Sculptures and three-dimensional artworks are placed in the loggia, which is equipped with a sidelight. Other rooms, such as the dining room and salon, are linked by the so-called promenade of art, their design continuing the palette of light surfaces, dark wooden furniture and mirrors.

The path linking the rooms is bordered on both sides by semi-permeable mirrors that afford glimpses but not a full view as long as the brightness of the vitrine is lighter than that of the room. With reference to Pistoletto, the oxidized silver is reflected to infinity. The white walls and floors are contrasted by black wallpaper in the salon where the TV is concealed within a magic mirrored bar.

Finally, the former orangery is dominated by a sculptural kitchen unit made of "wenge"-wood, its curved cladding continuing along the wall around the dining table and barbecue. Beneath it is space for smaller works of art, although culinary enjoyment among friends is certainly the focus of this area.

This spread | Kitchen

CLIENT | Private client
YEAR | 2014
SIZE | 389m²
STATUS | Built

PROJECT | Single-family house, loft

PITT STUDIO
LOS FELIZ | USA

This studio remodel for a Hollywood movie actor incorporates the clients' interest in multicultural architectonic references and his hybrid lifestyle.

The studio needs to accommodate living and working in one space and provide a means to shift flexibly between professional and private life. The true test of the studio's quality is its ability to adapt and be usable in the long-term, accommodating changing functional demands and creating different spatial possibilities. The solution to this problem shapes the aesthetic experience of the house.

The formal language of the studio translates the haptic material quality of an adjacent guest house into a fusion of traditional Japanese and European proportion systems. The studio grafts the Chigaidana of Japanese furniture with the European idea of the golden ratio. These 'genetic codes' infuse one another to create a new design language with its own syntactic, semantic and phenomenological components. While rooted in two different worlds, the formal expression becomes something new and independent, a Darwinistic evolution of aesthetic value systems into a robust 'genetic bastard'.

The studio responds to the patterns of multicultural urban life, effecting a flexible self-organizing, fluid balance between the poles of need and cultural heritage. It is a habitat that serves as a stage for the continuous re-allegorization of life.

Left | Studio space
Right | Bathroom

CLIENT | Brad Pitt
YEAR | 1998
SIZE | undisclosed
STATUS | Built
IN COLLABORATION WITH | Brad Pitt

PROJECT | Multi-family house, mixed use

TOR149
BERLIN | GERMANY

―――――

A new apartment building has arrived in Berlin-Mitte. Boldly designed, innovative and elegant, it is an avant-garde building-sculpture in the heart of Berlin that lies somewhere between bourgeois spaciousness and modern transparency. The building stands out with its prismatic aluminum façade, bright, sculptural lobby space and intelligent layout of the split-level apartments.

The innovative façade of TOR149 is an extraordinary visual highlight. Its crystalline surface reflects the sky over the city, changing in appearance with its exposure to light. As one walks past the building, one is accompanied by an ever-changing pattern of light and shadow caused by the material of the faceted façade elements reflecting light in different ways. The façade transforms the traditional qualities of stucco work and the historical proportions of window openings, giving the building a new look.

The house is a conciliatory gesture towards the emotionally-charged atmosphere of Berlin's ongoing stylistic discourse on nostalgia versus experimentation. The design of TOR149 neither neglects nor emulates historic heritage and urban context but instead attempts to be a continuation of Berlin's story. Above all, it presents a possible vision for a home of the future in Berlin. Instead of a classical façade, where the stucco relief is symmetrical about the center of the frontage, the prismatic relief of TOR149 is twisted to the east.

....

Right | Façade

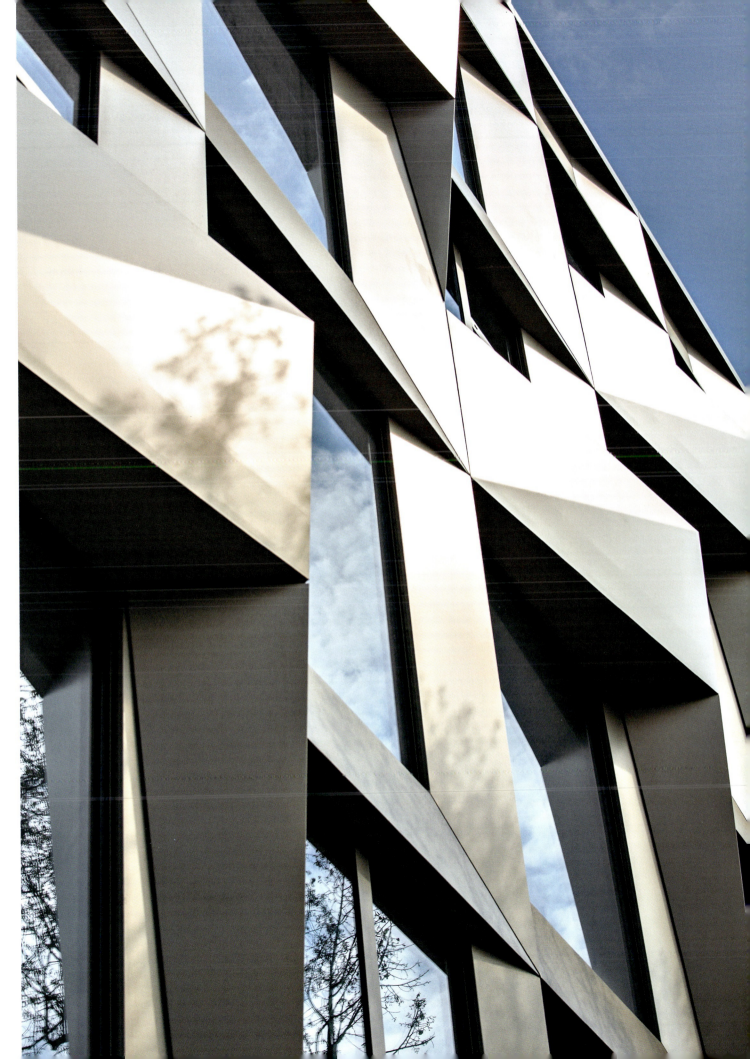

Left | Kitchen, split-level apartment
Right | Living room

....

Located at a slight bend in the Torstrasse, this produces a visual effect in which the building seems to "look" in both directions. Coming from east, the effect of the triangulated surface is sharp and narrow, but approaching the building from Friedrichstrasse, it seems wide and sharp. From one direction pedestrians experience the building as being contemporary and transparent, from the other as fitting into the closed frontage of historical Gründerzeit buildings.

TOR149 makes a new contribution to the planning of Berlin's public spaces by referring to tradition and addressing a desire for solid urban identity, as well as by bringing fresh, futuristic building back into the cosmopolitan city.

The split-level arrangement creates spacious interior experiences more reminiscent of single-family houses. An underground car park beneath the building and an inner courtyard of raised beds surrounded by natural stone round off the building's amenities. The apartments have underfloor heating supplied by a solar thermal energy and gas condensing boiler heating system, a house ventilation system with heat recovery, air-conditioning, a charging station for electric vehicles and an elevator.

———

This spread | 3D section and floor plans

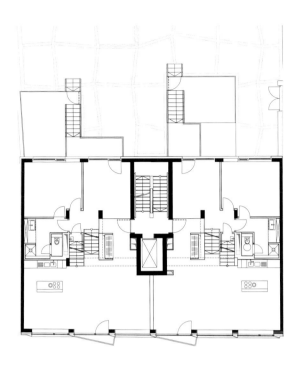

1st floor plan

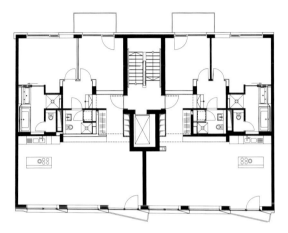

3rd floor plan

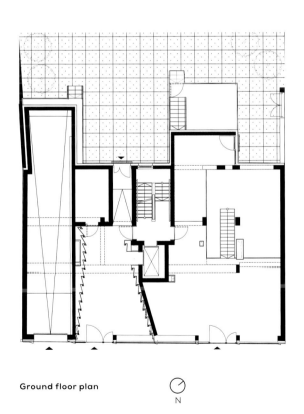

Ground floor plan

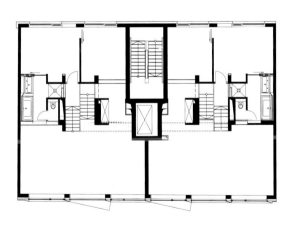

2nd floor plan

0 2 5 10 Meters

Left | Lobby
Right | Elevator

CLIENT | TOR149 Grundbesitz GmbH
YEAR | 2013
SIZE | 2,000m²
STATUS | Built

PROJECT | Residential tower, interior design

PANORAMA TOWERS
LAS VEGAS | USA

After decades of horizontal urban expansion and single-family residences, residential high-rise buildings began to mushroom in Las Vegas after the turn of the century. The Panorama Towers, one of the first such projects, broke ground in 2004 and were completed in 2007. GRAFT was commissioned to design all the public areas of this landmark project, and acted as design consultant for the overall aesthetics of the towers. GRAFT designed a dynamic façade with pronounced horizontal structure that reflects the idea of acceleration when passing by on the adjacent freeway.

The towers were also one of the first high-rise residential developments with a modern expression in Las Vegas. The dynamic horizontality of the façade creates generous open terrace spaces, affording stunning views of the strip and the desert landscape of Nevada.

The surrounding landscape of the desert, with its canyons, eroded creeks, Indian cave dwellings and oases, served as inspiration for the design of the extensive topography of the pool and leisure areas, situating modern living within its Nevada desert context.

CLIENT | Sasson Halier Investment
YEAR | 2007
SIZE | 111,000m²
STATUS | Built

PROJECT | Multi-family house, retail, mixed use

TEMPLINER STRASSE
BERLIN | GERMANY

The new complex of buildings at Teutoburger Platz is located in Berlin's popular Prenzlauer Berg district and completes the corner of an urban block. The complex comprises two buildings on each street, two in the courtyard and a prominent corner building.

The ground floor contains only commercial functions with a supermarket occupying the corner site, serving the local neighborhood. The upper storeys from the first to sixth floor comprise a mix of small to medium-sized apartments with between two and five rooms. Carefully designed floor plans ensure that all apartments are bright and spacious and can be used flexibly. Some of the larger 80-90m² apartments feature an intelligent, flexible utility block with bathroom in the center of the floor plan. The larger apartments and penthouses on the upper floors have fantastic views over the greenery in the Teutoburger Platz. Overall, the complex comprises 107 dwellings, two commercial units along with underground parking.

The façades of the five street-facing buildings are articulated with a mix of projecting surfaces and indented loggias. The buildings, while demonstratively modern, blend into the overall pattern of the neighborhood. The courtyard in the block interior is planted with trees, creating a green space within. The range of different apartment types and sizes ensures a mix of different residents.

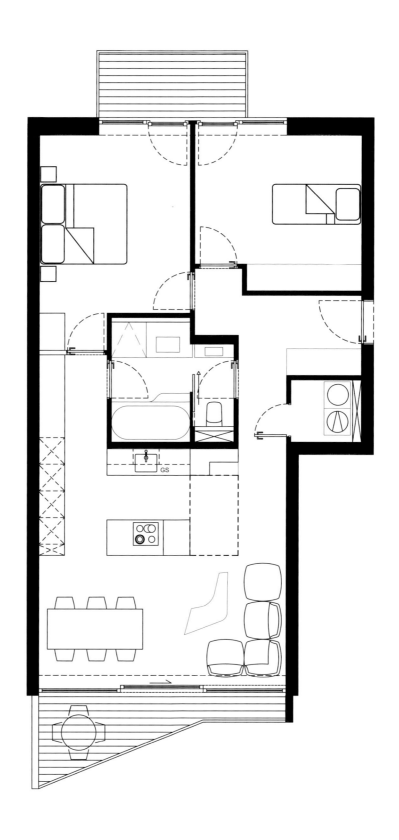

Floor plan Berlin II apartment

CLIENT | Bewocon GmbH
YEAR | 2018
SIZE | 21,00m²
STATUS | Under construction

PROJECT | Loft, apartment

LOFT HAUSVOGTEIPLATZ
BERLIN | GERMANY

The interior design of this Berlin loft is characterized by the dynamic lines of the open, bright space and the shape of the custom-made dark cubes.

All intimate and serving spaces, such as bathrooms, the dressing room and kitchen, are situated within or around the cubes, which additionally zone the space, obviating the need to subdivide the loft with walls. The wooden surfaces of the cubes and their visual separation from the walls and ceilings give them the character of items of furniture. The axes of the loggias towards the square in front of the building form the starting point for the dynamics of the flowing interior. In order not to compromise the clear, sharp lines of the cubes, all paintings or power outlets were integrated flush into the walls of the cubes.

The staircase from the loft to the upper floor/roof terrace is decorated with an individual ceiling mural.

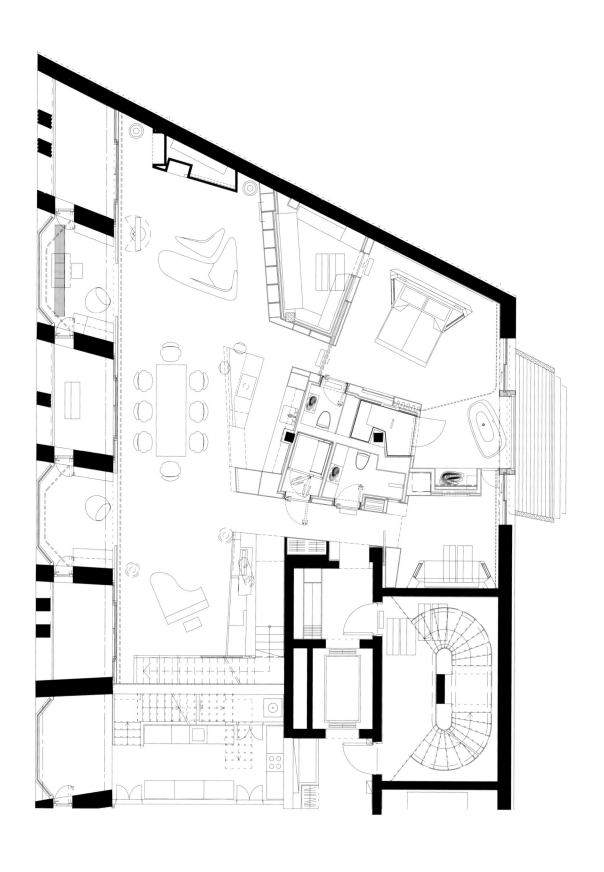

Floor plan

Right | Mirrored staircase in the living area

CLIENT | Privat client
YEAR | 2012
SIZE | 308m²
STATUS | Built

PROJECT | Single-family house, villa

VILLA M
BERLIN | GERMANY

GRAFT's design for a private villa in Berlin's venerable Grunewald quarter presents a striking, modern interpretation of comfortable living in the city. It's trapezoidal, sculptural form and modern architectural language symbolizes a boulder in a glacial landscape and differentiates it from its neighbors. The distinctive, three-dimensional figure of the four-storey building appears to rise out of the ground. For its design, GRAFT abstracted the classical rules of villa design and digitally synthesized them with natural phenomena shifting the tectonics of a villa towards those of a sculpture.

The façade is clad with ceramic plates that reinforce the impression of a large stone boulder. Horizontal incisions in the faceted surface of the façade for the loggias and floor-to-ceiling glazing are strategically placed to establish visual connections with the surrounding greenery while maintaining privacy. This asymmetrical appearance is reflected in the interiors where flowing transitions between the rooms create a sense of openness. The internal stairs and fireplace, in particular, break with residential design conventions. The centerpiece of the house is the living room, a prismatic, spacious open space designed for maximum comfort.

....

....

Aside from the kitchen and the living room, there are two additional rooms on the ground floor, a master bedroom on the upper floor as well as a large corridor, terrace and four further rooms. The top floor is a self-contained flat that can be used flexibly. The entrance, double garage, storage spaces and a spa are located on the lower ground floor. Travertine stone flooring also reinforces associations with a boulder.

The floor plans are designed to be flexible, so that they can adapt to the residents' changing life situations. Floors can be separated off into self-contained apartments, accessed via the outer staircase. The materials were chosen for durability and recyclability and heat is provided by a geothermal system. The orientation of the building is optimized for energy efficiency and the building's energy performance is better than current energy conservation legislation demands.

———

CLIENT | Private client
YEAR | 2016
SIZE | 870m²
STATUS | Under construction

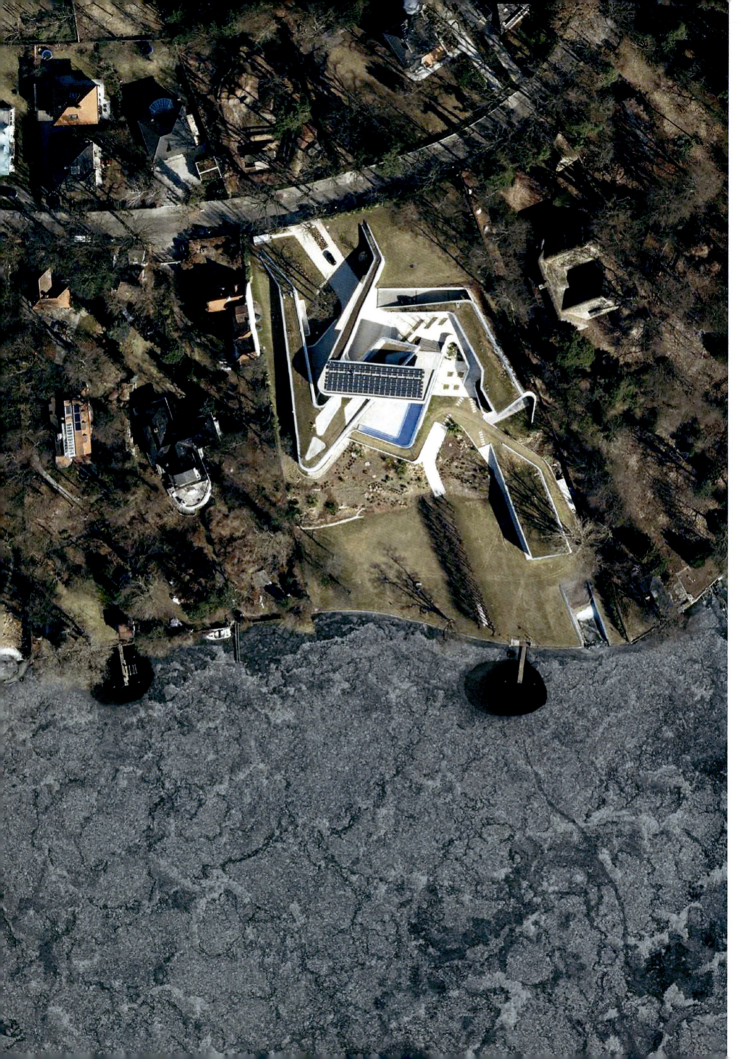

PROJECT | Single-family house, villa

LAKESIDE VILLA BERLIN
BERLIN | GERMANY

Positioned on a bluff overlooking a beautiful lake to the southwest, the villa's design draws on the genius loci of its location.

The appearance of the villa has been kept intentionally modest, so that it fits into the surrounding landscape. The villa is therefore divided into three main sections, each rising from the topography as one progresses towards the street. The three separate forms appear to embrace one another, creating a natural dynamic flow of space that guides visitors deeper into the site and the lake beyond. The design both benefits from and enhances the qualities of its location. The floor plans of the main building sections likewise intersect, creating interesting spatial and functional intersections.

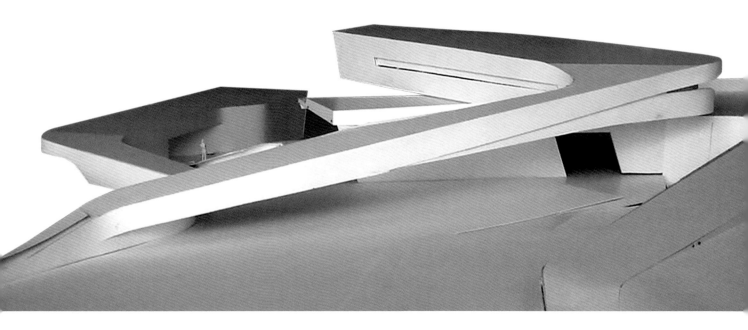

Left | Physical model Lakeside villa

YEAR | 2011
STATUS | Built

PROJECT | Multi-family house

WAVE
BERLIN | GERMANY

GRAFT's design for WAVE, a new residential complex on the site of the former eastern harbor on the Spree River in Berlin, maximizes the potential of its waterfront location. Two apartment buildings face the river either side of an inner courtyard.

All apartments look out over the water with spectacular views over the river, the iconic sculpture "Molecule Man" by Jonathan Borofsky and the districts of Kreuzberg, Friedrichshain and Treptow beyond. All units on the waterfront face south, making the most of the sun.

The building's sculptural expression derives from the flowing motion of the water, with smooth rounded corners and arcing, organic balconies. On the street side, the façade is punctuated by bay windows and balconies. The buildings contain a variety of different apartment types and sizes to achieve a mix of tenants and target groups. They range from 1.5 room apartments of 27 – 47m², to two- to five-room apartments of between 44 and 156m². Mezzanine apartments have private gardens and the top floor contains luxurious five- to six-room penthouses of 206 – 296m² with private access to a roof garden. The majority of the 161 apartments have either a balcony or a bay window.

The rooftop is conceived as a "fifth façade" with green gardens and lounge areas. There are two additional rooftop spaces. Together with the lush courtyard in the communal atrium, the project is a green oasis in the heart of the city.

CLIENT | Private client
YEAR | 2016
SIZE | 12,000m²
STATUS | Under construction

PROJECT | Single-family house, refurbishment of a Baroque Palais

ALMSTADTSTRASSE
BERLIN | GERMANY

GRAFT designed and planned the restoration of a listed Baroque Palais in Berlin's Mitte district. The interior design follows a mnemonic concept: modern architectural insertions create a narrative throughout the building, blending smooth, metallic materials respectfully into the historic, textured and profiled building structure.

In response to the historical lime plaster, other parts of the interior are built using modern earthen materials. What begins as small detailed insertions culminates in a completely modern loft conversion on the top floor. The numerous historical details and objects in combination with the modern insertions create an exciting frisson, the new framing the old, encoding the traces of memory.

The common areas are designed for maximum flexibility and openness. A home office and guest apartment have been incorporated into the loft conversion and the rear façade opens onto a spacious private outdoor area.

Left | Entrance area

Left bottom | Kitchen and living room
Right | Bathroom

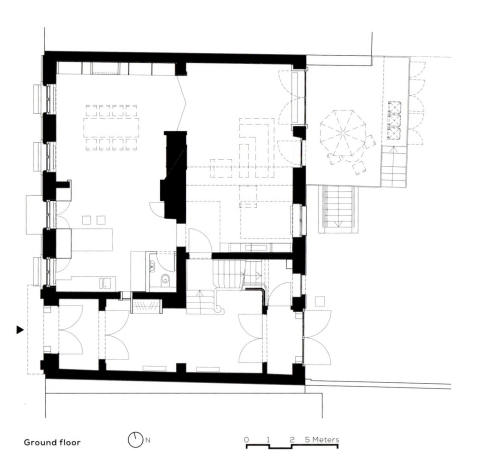

Ground floor   N   0 1 2 5 Meters

Left | Spacious wardrobe
Right | Loft conversion on the top floor

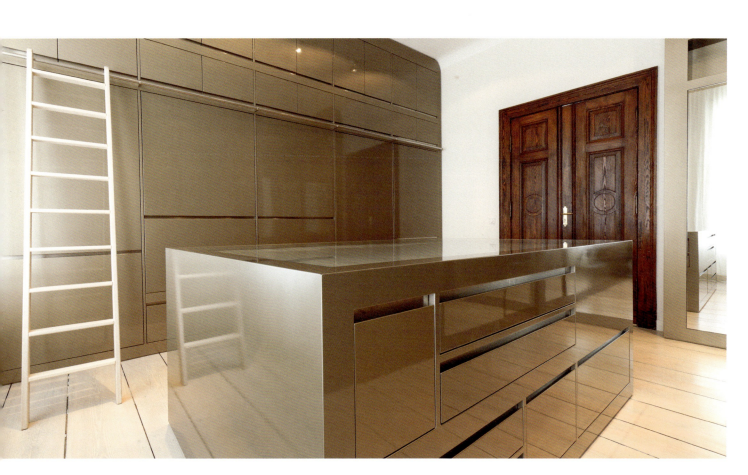

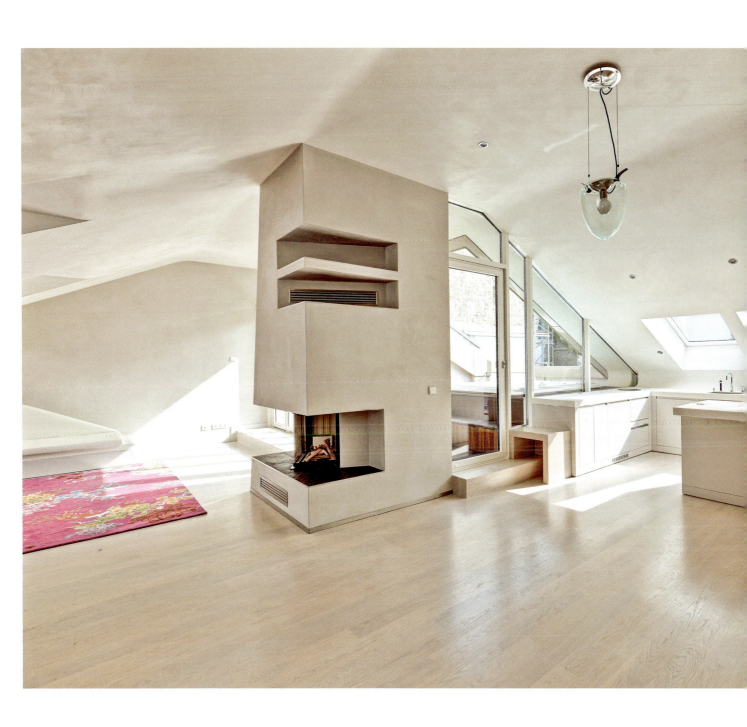

CLIENT | Private client
YEAR | 2011
SIZE | 510m²
STATUS | Built

PROJECT | Loft, apartment

LOFT HAMBURG
HAMBURG | GERMANY

As with all renovations, the existing building services and structure had to be incorporated in the overall design. This was achieved through the use of a free-standing walnut unit which functions as the heart of the apartment. This unit incorporates the kitchen, bathroom and dresser, taking advantage of its proximity to the building services. Sections are cut out of the unit to allow natural light to penetrate deep into the loft. Flanking the walnut core are service walls contrasted in white. These walls house the rest of the functional elements of the space, embedded within niches so that the remaining space can be used flexibly for working, relaxation, bathing and sleeping. Further flexibility is achieved through the use of ceiling-high, room-dividing sliding walls that allow the relationship of public and private space within the loft to be configured as needed. The sliding walls, when retracted, are completely concealed within the service walls.

Left top | Free-standing walnut unit with kitchen, bathroom and dresser

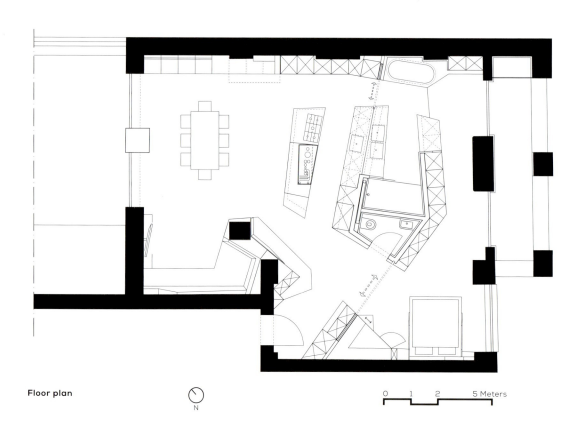

Floor plan

Left | Bathtub
Right | Walnut unit

CLIENT | Private client
YEAR | 2009
SIZE | 120m²
STATUS | Built

PROJECT | Single-family house, villa

VILLA J
SOUTHERN ENGLAND | UNITED KINGDOM

In southern England, GRAFT designed an ambitious house that blends into its surrounding landscape but is nevertheless an architectural statement.

The concept of the proposed building derives from the idea and character of the place itself. Located on a slight south-facing slope, the new architecture embraces the nature of the site and the landscape of the South Downs. The soil, for example, will be used to create rammed earth walls that support the roof structure. The green roof visually embeds the building in its surroundings but also retains rainwater, filtering and collecting it for grey water usage.

The building is shielded to the north and opens to the south to reveal a panoramic view over the Downs and the sun's celestial path. Passive house strategies help reduce energy demand by embedding the house in the ground to the north and opening it to the south to allow the low sun in winter to penetrate the house and warm it naturally. Roof overhangs avoid heat gains from the high sun during summer.

The energy concept is likewise woven into the fabric of the agricultural landscape. Two lines of photovoltaic panels will be added to the rows of vines behind the house. Just as the vines convert the sun's energy into fructose, the photovoltaic cells will use the sun to supply the house with clean energy. A geothermal system will be used to heat the house. The water system minimizes water consumption using low flow fixtures, rain water recycling and grey water recycling from the pool and wash hand basins for WC flushing.

Although the volume of the house is embedded in the landscape, the house is distinctive and individual in its design, even on the north side. The roof line never actually touches the ground and from close-up, the building itself is perceived as a distinct architectural entity.

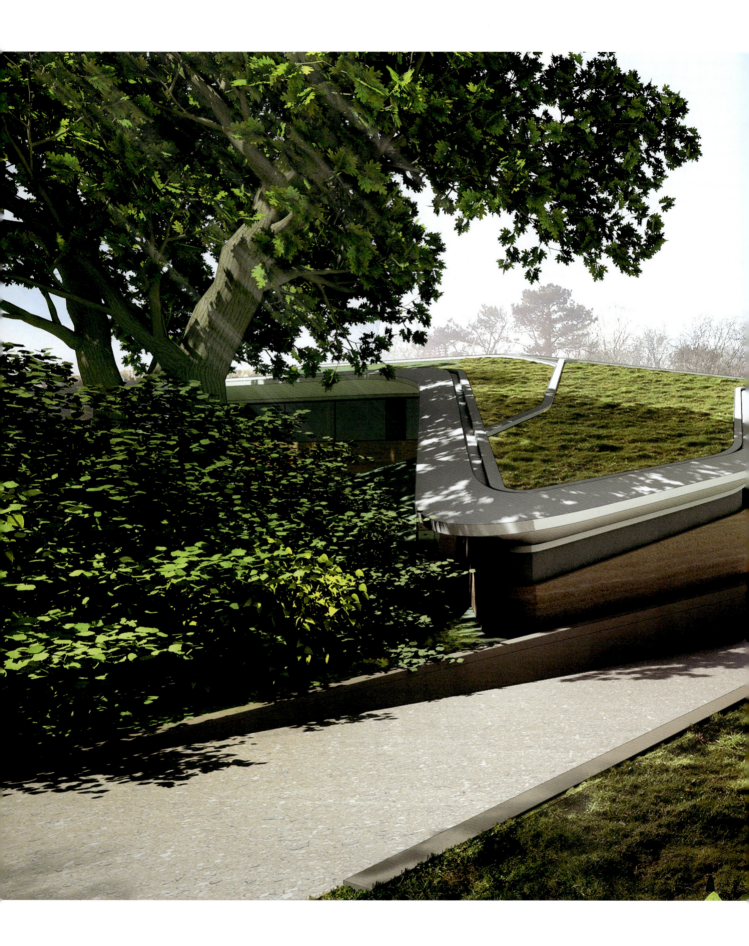

This spread | Driveway and entrance area

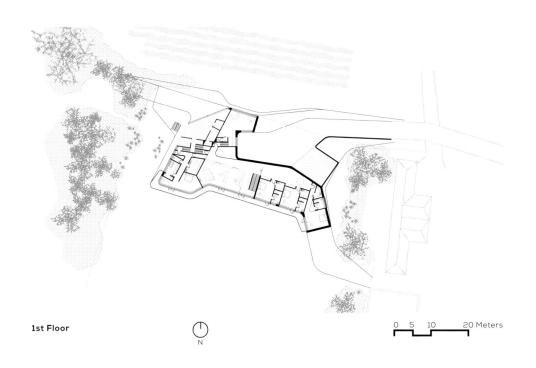

1st Floor

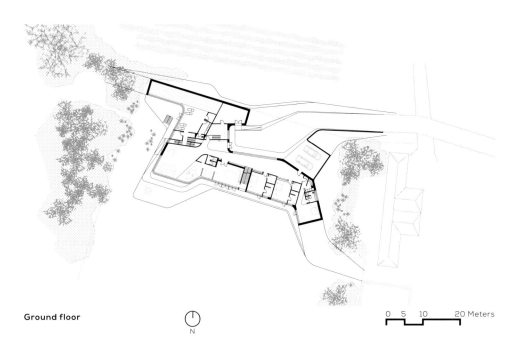

Ground floor

CLIENT | Private client
YEAR | 2015
SIZE | 700m²
STATUS | In progress

PROJECT | Loft, apartment

LOFT GLEIMSTRASSE
BERLIN | GERMANY

———

Living and working, openness and intimacy – flexibility has become a key concept in contemporary loft design. Lofts are usually closed off from "the public eye" or guests, allowing residents to create their own hidden worlds. Spaces can be open and fluid, transitioning from bedroom to bathroom and living room to kitchen. The degree of individual expression is limited only by the imagination of the resident.

The transformation of the upper story of a typical 19th century building in one of Berlin's hip residential areas stages an interplay between private and public space. A substantial part of the floor space remains open and is rarely furnished. Intimate and service spaces – bathrooms, closets, store rooms, stairs and entrances – are integrated and concealed within a sculptural "mega form" carved out of the space that defines the various regions of the domicile. The contrasting qualities of the dense central block and the flowing space around it create both sheltered "cave-like" and open "stage-like" atmospheres. Sliding walls facilitate spatial subdivisions around the core: bedrooms and adjacent bathrooms may be combined into suites, and space may be claimed alternately for extroverted or introverted uses.

The kitchen, the loft's central element, is clad entirely in high-quality concrete plaster, giving it the effect of having been carved out of a massive block. The walls and sculptural interior are fashioned as a sophisticated drywall

....

Right | Open living room with built-in seating area

Left | Bedroom
Right | Bathroom with sliding doors

construction, and incorporate beds, benches, sofas, walk-in closets, shelves, and a library. Nooks and cut-outs in the resulting volume invite one to inhabit surrounding walls.

Two 13-meter-wide balconies visually extend the interior space on both sides of the loft and offer a spectacular panorama of the Berlin skyline. The north and south façades are glazed and can be folded back completely to allow the interior to extend outwards. A roof garden above looks out over Berlin.

———

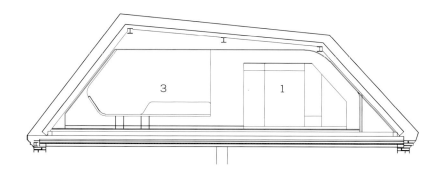

Section AA

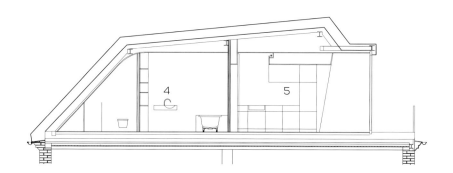

Section BB

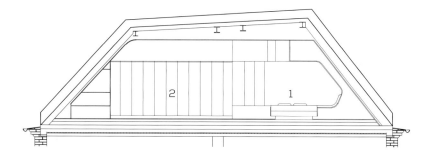

Section CC

1. Sleeping
2. Wardrobe
3. Sitting
4. Lavatory
5. Kitchen

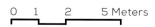

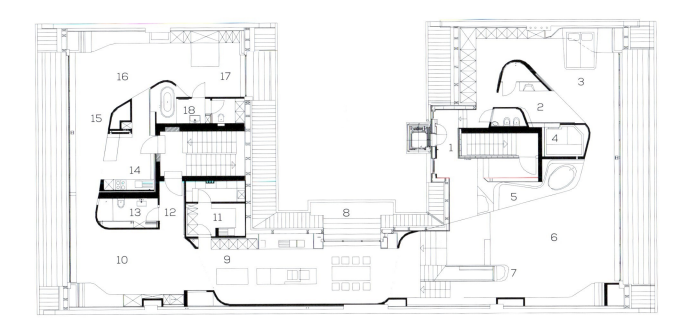

Floor plan

1. Entrance
2. Bathroom
3. Bedroom
4. Sauna
5. Sitting niche
6. Living area
7. Fireplace
8. Terrace
9. Kitchen
10. Working area
11. Pantry
12. Entrance
13. Lavatory
14. Kitchen
15. Fireplace
16. Living area
17. Sleeping
18. Bathroom

0 1 2 5 Meters

Top | Fireplace
Left bottom | Kitchen
Right bottom | Living room

CLIENT | Private client
TIME | 2005
SIZE | 350m²
STATUS | Built

PROJECT | Housing solution for refugees in Europe

HEIMAT2
BERLIN | GERMANY

Worldwide displacement and refugee movements hit an all-time high in 2016 with 60 million people forced to leave their homes and seek asylum elsewhere. In Germany in particular, asylum claims reached a historic high with 442,000 first applications in 2015 – a 155% increase over the year before. Just at a time when Germany is facing its first home-made housing crisis since the re-unification, the influx of refugees puts authorities under further pressure.

GRAFT co-founded Heimat2 with partners Comterra Care, Lepi Ventures, Bernstein Group and H.W. Pausch to provide dignified housing solutions for refugees in Germany that combine short- and long-term solutions from typical disaster relief programs. The objective is to build model residential villages that are socially inclusive and provide living environments of the best possible standard. Apart from long-term tasks, the immediate goal is to provide shelter and the perspective of a more permanent living situation
Looking at the urgent challenge, Heimat2 reacts with fast and present solutions for accommodation within modular construction systems - with the best possible conditions for the inhabitants and residents.

In close collaboration with well-known charity organizations, Heimat2 invented a holistic concept that offers excellent operators, communication on site and the opportunity to flexibly enlarge the residential villages or later re-use them for another purpose.

Left | Community courtyard

Site plan N

0 5 10 20 Meters

CLIENT | Heimat2
YEAR | 2016
STATUS | In progress

PROJECT | Co-founding Make It Right Foundation, masterplanning, design for single-family houses

MAKE IT RIGHT
NEW ORLEANS | USA

Hurricane Katrina, which hit the Gulf Coast in 2005, was one of the deadliest hurricanes in the USA, and the costliest disaster in the world so far. The entire district of the Lower Ninth Ward in New Orleans lies below sea level and was completely destroyed and its population displaced. A year after the catastrophe, nothing had been done and residents could not return to rebuild their homes and neighborhoods. Brad Pitt visited the area while shooting a movie and decided something had to be done.

In 2007, GRAFT started the "Make It Right Foundation" (MIR) together with Brad Pitt, Bill McDonough and the Cherokee Foundation to rebuild the Lower 9th Ward. In order to raise funds and create awareness, the foundation designed the Pink Project to officially launch the rebuilding efforts and prepare the first round of financing after Brad Pitt's initial donation. Using an approach that blends set design and architecture, 150 pink scaffolding structures were erected on the site that was still empty two years after the floods. These structures served as placeholders for future buildings and building parts and acted as a compelling tool to raise awareness. Over time, as monetary donations came in, the pink placeholders were reassembled to resurrect the urban pattern of the community before the disaster.

Over the course of many months, Pitt, GRAFT and the other parties involved met with former homeowners and local community leaders. GRAFT took on the role of an architectural curator on the board of MIR and invited a group of 21 architects to create a range of architectural solutions.

....

Right | Street perspective Lower 9th Ward

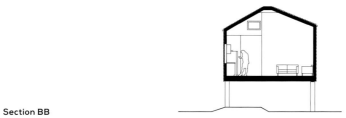
Section BB

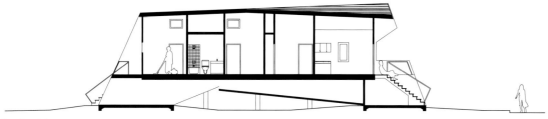
Section AA

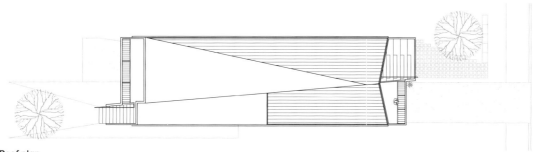
Roof plan

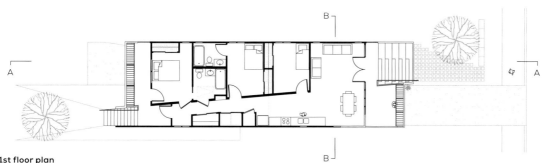
1st floor plan

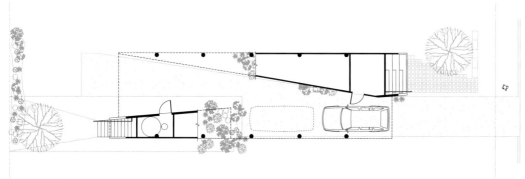
Ground floor plan

0 1 2 5 Meters

....

GRAFT also contributed two designs for affordable, sustainable and safe houses based on popular dwelling typologies and the rich traditions of New Orleans. Sustainability strategies follow the cradle-to-cradle principle established by William McDonough and Michael Braungart. This and other efforts contributed to reducing energy demand, lowering monthly utility costs from up to US$ 300 before Katrina to only US$ 25 per month. Make It Right designed a catalog of houses with diverse styles but similar floor spaces and prices. The residents could then choose the house they wanted. All architects volunteered their time and designs for the community to create a sustainable, climate-responsive and diverse neighborhood. To date, more than 100 homes have been built, all of which have earned LEED Platinum status, making it the largest community in the USA with this certificate. More than 350 people now live in Make It Right homes.

....

…………

Graft's proposal for housing merges metaphorical abstractions of traditional and modern architecture, drawing on the more successful components of each to create a new, robust whole. Our proposal began with a traditional New Orleans house type, the shot gun house, which is abstractly represented through an expressive, almost exaggerated gable roof and generous front porch. The fluidity of the relationship between home and community, and the provision of areas designed for interaction with neighbors and friends, is one of the things that makes the Lower Ninth so incredibly special. We felt it important to pay homage to this. These traditional typological elements are coupled with modern, affordable, sustainable amenities. The cross-section of the house transitions progressively towards the rear of the house, beginning as a traditional frontage facing the street and ending as a flat-roofed modern, rectilinear building at the back. This flat roof also doubles as a safe haven that the residents can flee to in the event of another flood.

The building's sustainable features include: Solar panels, water catchment system, a geothermal system with heat pump, tankless water heating, high ceilings for stack ventilation, operable windows which assist stack ventilation and cross ventilation, highly insulated hurricane resistant windows, High-R-value insulation, no off-gassing paints and finishing materials, permeable paving, energy star appliances, ceiling fans, and low-flow toilets.

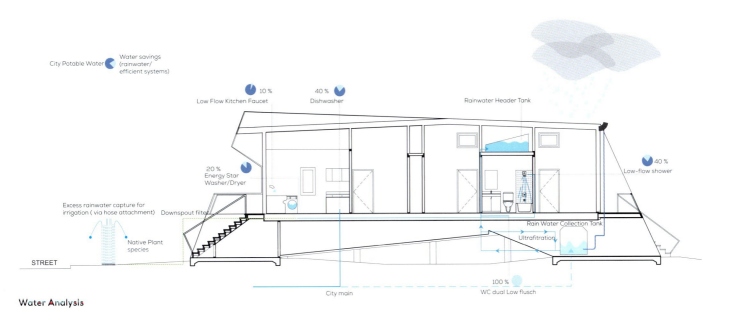

Water Analysis

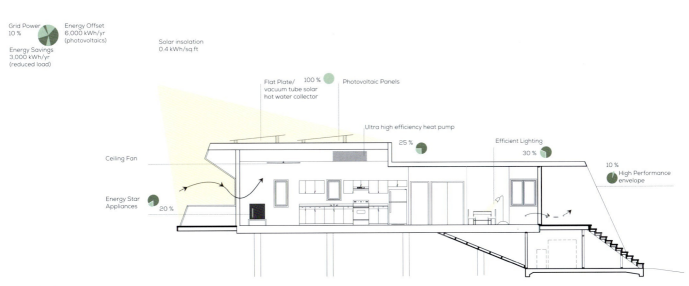

Energy Analysis

CLIENT | Make It Right Foundation **YEAR |** 2006-2008
SIZE | 100m² - 300m² / house
STATUS | Built, ongoing
IN COLLABORATION WITH | Brad Pitt, William McDonough, Tom Darden II, Tom Darden III

PROJECT | Prototypical urban planning of 1,000 housing units

NAMIBIA AFFORDABLE HOUSING
ONGWEDIVA, ONDANGWA & WALVIS BAY I NAMIBIA

Namibia is experiencing a housing crisis. Strategies currently employed to reduce the backlog are proving ineffective. Increasing demand escalates prices, meanwhile the country's rapid urbanization maintains a steady influx of low wage earners from rural areas seeking better opportunities in urban areas. The newcomers are greeted by too few rental offers, at too high a cost, resulting in the majority of rural-urban migrants living in shacks on the outskirts of cities.

Housing policies in Namibia favor single story detached housing sitting on a minimum 300m² plot of land, requiring a great deal of land to be levelled and serviced at high cost, but benefiting few. Additionally, zoning practices keep residential and commercial uses separate, resulting in an urban sprawl which forces people to either live hours of commute from jobs and job opportunities, or to rent informal shacks in the underused gardens of those living closer to urban centers. Within these informal settlements however, the highly entrepreneurial residents have created a second, informal job market, so that one finds several businesses at every junction.

Our design seeks to provide a model for provision of housing that reverses the trend of unaffordable and unsustainable development, by reducing the costs involved in the construction of housing and providing a structure for future growth and activity within the new neighborhoods. We identified three key design elements for achieving this:

....

This spread | Masterplan Walvis Bay

Left top | Townhouses
Left bottom | Courtyard houses
Right bottom | Apartment buildings

Densification: reducing the plot size of the houses to reduce the amount of serviced land and related costs for each unit, as well as reducing construction material by using housing typologies which have shared construction elements (i.e. attached housing and apartments).

Mixed-use: to provide a hybrid architecture, which facilitates using the home for business at varying scales.

Incremental housing: using modular elements that allow a compact core to extend vertically and/or horizontally in a cost efficient manner.
These key elements, Densification, Mixed-use, and Incremental housing, as well as the particular climate of Namibia, led to the development of three typologies: townhouses, courtyard houses and apartments. The typologies are designed so that they can be combined to create an urbanscape as vibrant and inviting as the community that grows within it.

The built-in cost efficiencies open up a potential market for private developers within the low-cost sector, which was previously only approached by subsidized housing programs that failed miserably. Making low-cost housing units not only affordable but profitable is the only realistic and sustainable answer for a solution desperately needed on a large scale - the prime objective of the cooperation of GRAFT together with KfW.

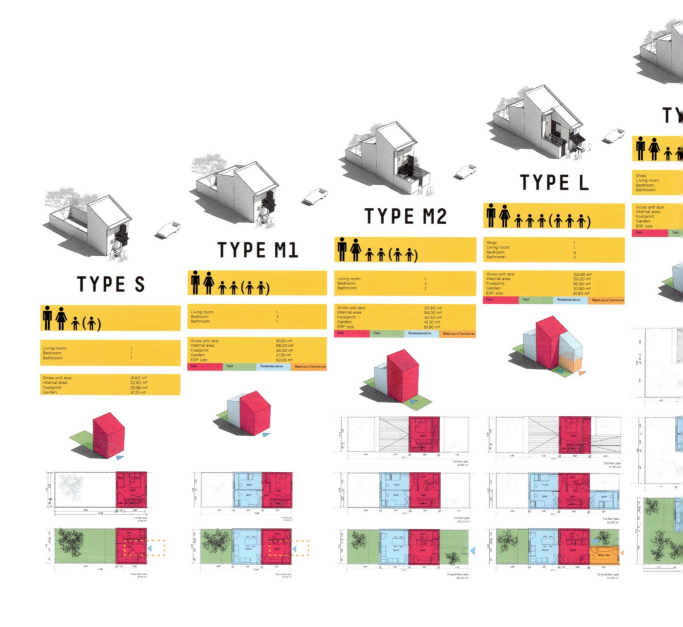

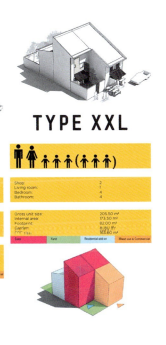

TYPE XXL

CLIENT | KfW Development Bank
YEAR | 2013
SIZE | 32,700 – 42,750m²
SIZE HOUSING UNITS | 41m² apartments – 205m² housing units
STATUS | In progress
PARTNER | German Embassy Namibia
NAMIBIAN CONSULTANTS | Nina Maritz Architects, Emcon Consulting Engineers, WML Consulting Engineers, DE LEEUW

PROJECT | Masterplanning, single-family houses

TELTOWN
TELTOW | GERMANY

In the small town of Teltow south of Berlin, GRAFT designed and planned a residential district named TelTown, consisting of 91 single-family houses that offer green living with an urban character. Teltow is well situated in close proximity to the urban vibrancy of the capital but also in remarkable natural surroundings.

The house types have been carefully designed and adjusted to suit the needs of diverse residents. The roof forms and internal configurations vary, and some houses have extensions to meet different living requirements. These individual variations avoid monotony and help to create an open and lively district. In addition to the private gardens, numerous other green spaces and small public meeting areas and playing fields provide opportunities for neighbors to interact.

A holistic energy concept protects the local environment while ensuring a constant supply of energy without creating excessive costs. Similarly, attention was given to choosing suitably ecological building materials.

A total of 91 terraced two- or three-story houses and a single semi-detached house were built in Teltow with floor areas ranging from 77m² to 180m².

GRAFT's innovative approach in TelTown marries innovative design with multi-disciplinary construction principles, setting new standards for housing projects.

CLIENT | CD Deutsche Eigenheim AG
YEAR | 2012
SIZE | 27,100m²
STATUS | Built

PROJECT | Multi-family house, mixed use, refurbishment, new construction

BRICKS BERLIN SCHÖNEBERG
BERLIN | GERMANY

GRAFT was commissioned to develop the new BRICKS complex on the grounds of the former Postfuhramt (post office) between Hauptstrasse and Belziger Strasse in Berlin Schöneberg close to Acacia Kiez. The ensemble is a mixed-use complex of new buildings and renovated historical buildings with three courtyards partially linked by a public passage that connects them to the vibrant heart of Berlin's Schöneberg district.

The design of the new building picks up the materiality of the historical buildings (dating from 1900 to 1928) reinterpreting their brickwork façades in a new, contemporary form.

The brick facing undulates softly at the top and bottom like fabric to create a sense of sculptural depth, at the bottom receding inwards to draw people from the street into the passage to the courtyard.

To begin with, part of the area will be made publicly accessible and then successively redeveloped in stages. The unused roof spaces of the post office and boiler house will be converted for commercial use, then the roofs of the side wings and cross wing (damaged during World War II) rebuilt and converted into offices. The provisional roof of the switching exchange, erected during the war, will be dismantled and likewise converted for commercial use.

....

Left | Entrance area

Left | Façade Belziger Strasse

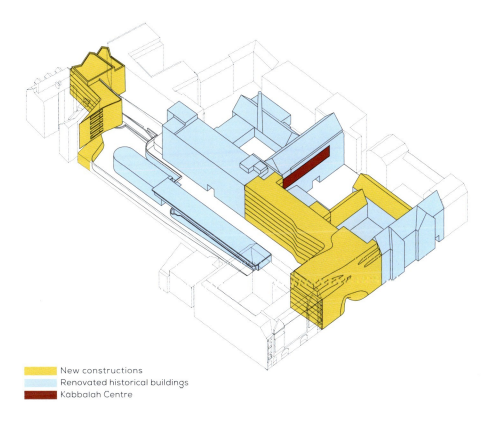

New constructions
Renovated historical buildings
Kabbalah Centre

....

GRAFT's design envisages a total of 128 new apartments, 107 on the Hauptstrasse and 21 on the Belziger Strasse, along with 35 commercial units for offices, retail and restaurants, as well as a primary school, spaces for the university, a taekwondo school and Kabbalah Centre.

The Kabbalah Centre was completed in 2015 and occupies a 7.5m-high space on the third floor that originally served as a telegraph switching exchange. GRAFT's concept uses one of the central ideas of the teaching of Kabbalah of gradual perception as spatial development along a path. It also interconnects all the space from the entrance up to a flexible lecture hall and a generous staircase to a second level that appears to float freely inside the hall. A giant mirror on the rear wall visually extends the space, the reflected rhythm of the arches causing the space to appear twice as deep.

The entire development is based around a concept of respectful interaction between old and new and the completion of the existing ensemble, making contemporary use of the traditional brick material.

This spread | Apartment interiors

This spread | Interior Kabbalah Centre, built in 2015

CLIENT | Trockland
YEAR | 2015
SIZE | 32,000m²
STATUS | Under construction

PROJECT | Multi-family house, mixed use

CHARLIE LIVING
BERLIN | GERMANY

Charlie Living is the first block of a new ensemble of buildings that will repair many of the gaps around Checkpoint Charlie on Friedrichstrasse in central Berlin.

The first section, a block with 241 flats and 48 serviced apartments, takes a different approach to conventional courtyards and creates a public green space in the center that branches off the public urban areas as the focus for all four of the surrounding buildings. The space becomes part of the network of passages passing through the urban blocks and serves as a tranquil common space for the residents, shielded from traffic and tourists.
The section on Zimmerstrasse comprises apartments for rent with a common room and reception, along with an apartment hotel, shops and a restaurant. Its two-story, slightly recessed plinth picks up the line of the adjacent historical buildings and frames a glazed section that picks up the height of the former Berlin Wall at this point. This transparent, almost invisible structure becomes a connecting element that expresses the optimism and cosmopolitan character of the city after the fall of the Berlin Wall.

The garden, planted with domestic and non-native plants, also extends to the westward façade of the building in the form of a row of planted trees on the façade. A roof garden completes this hybrid "garden city" in the heart of Berlin.

Right | Street perspective

This spread | Courtyard and public green spaces

CLIENT | Trockland
YEAR | 2016
SIZE | 33,200m²
STATUS | Under construction

PROJECT | Masterplanning, single-family houses, multi-family houses, mixed use

BLÜTENVIERTEL
CAPUTH | GERMANY

In Caputh near Potsdam, GRAFT has developed a masterplan for a new residential area with a total of 105 housing units comprising a mix of single- and multi-family houses as well as apartment buildings.

The redevelopment extends the small-scale urban fabric of the town, respecting its mixed structure while adding new infrastructure and retail facilities. High-quality town houses and detached houses with gardens are complemented by apartment buildings with affordable housing to achieve a mix of residents and dwelling sizes. The park-like environment of the site has been maintained with small squares and green spaces within the site. Residents can also make use of the nearby recreational areas of the Schlosspark in Caputh and the lake. The new center of the neighborhood faces the water and ferry quayside.

GRAFT's concept also adds infrastructure and retail facilities that benefit the town as a whole. A supermarket was built in 2014 with an adjoining square that can be used as needed for parking or as a market square for market stalls and fairs.

Brick is used as a material to unify the different elements of the site and is applied in different patterns and structures for the paths and façades. This reflects the region's brick-making tradition, which played a major role in the Gründerzeit at the end of the 19th century, and the colour of the brick also anchors the project in the locality.

This spread | Squares and green spaces within the site

CLIENT | Dr. Lothar Hardt
YEAR | 2017
SIZE | 22,500m²
STATUS | In progress

PROJECT | Masterplanning, single-family houses, mixed use

AUENFLÜGEL
BERLIN | GERMANY

As part of the development of the northern Ahrensfelder Chaussee on the outskirts of Berlin, GRAFT planned a new residential district that will provide space for up to 2,200 people in 750 housing units. GRAFT developed three housing typologies that refer to the site's green, rural surroundings: peripheral, field and square developments. A mix of symmetrical and asymmetrical façades creates coherence while still maintaining a sense of variety.

The design process paid special attention to the specific qualities of the site, drawing inspiration from its natural surroundings, for example Lake Gehresee and the public park nearby. GRAFT's design for the new urban district builds on this potential, giving the Auenflügel quarter (English: meadow wings) a specific urban character infused by nature. The circular arrangement ensures that there are numerous pockets of nature within the district.

The urban figure comprises two distinct wings with clear peripheral and core developments. The housing typologies are grouped into peripheral, sectional and square developments, with the buildings on the periphery forming an urban edge, their interiors oriented around an inner garden. The green areas within the Auenflügel are interlinked and every house has its own small front garden for added privacy. Split-level floor plans create flexible yet private spaces and allow daylight to shine deep into the houses via the patios.

....

Right | Street perspective

This spread | Peripheral development

....

Within the Auenflügel, the houses offer a mix of regular and individual configurations. A modular system was developed for the roof construction to enable flexible extensions, and the different types of construction help create the impression of differential growth as opposed to instant uniformity. This flexible mix of types and configurations creates a sense of unity through diversity.

The road and path network of the Auenflügel district combines road infrastructure for car access with a network of small pedestrian and cycle paths that pass through the entire neighborhood. These small paths incorporate places to sit and enjoy the surroundings or interact with neighbors. The streets and paths sew together the entire district and provide pedestrian access to its shopping facilities and kindergarten.

―――

―――

CLIENT | CD Deutsche Eigenheim AG
YEAR | 2012
SIZE | 16,000m²
STATUS | In progress

―――

PROJECT | Single-family house

HAUS KOCH
BERLIN | GERMANY

The single-family house in Berlin-Biesdorf has two main floors, a sub-level, and a carport area. The living area extends across five different spaces in a split-level arrangement. The L-shape of the building is defined by the property lines at the north and east of the site and the roof drops downwards continually from its highest point on the northwest corner. From the street, the building appears sleek and unobtrusive, its forward face aligning with the neighboring buildings while its sides taper back to the rear. At the back, the house opens onto the garden, the space of the interior living area continuing out into the garden. The sculptural block of the building has L-shaped windows that span across the corners and extend partially up to the roof. While the openings to the street and on the north are minimal, the southern face features large floor-to-ceiling windows that open onto the garden.

Left | Living room with floor-to-ceiling windows

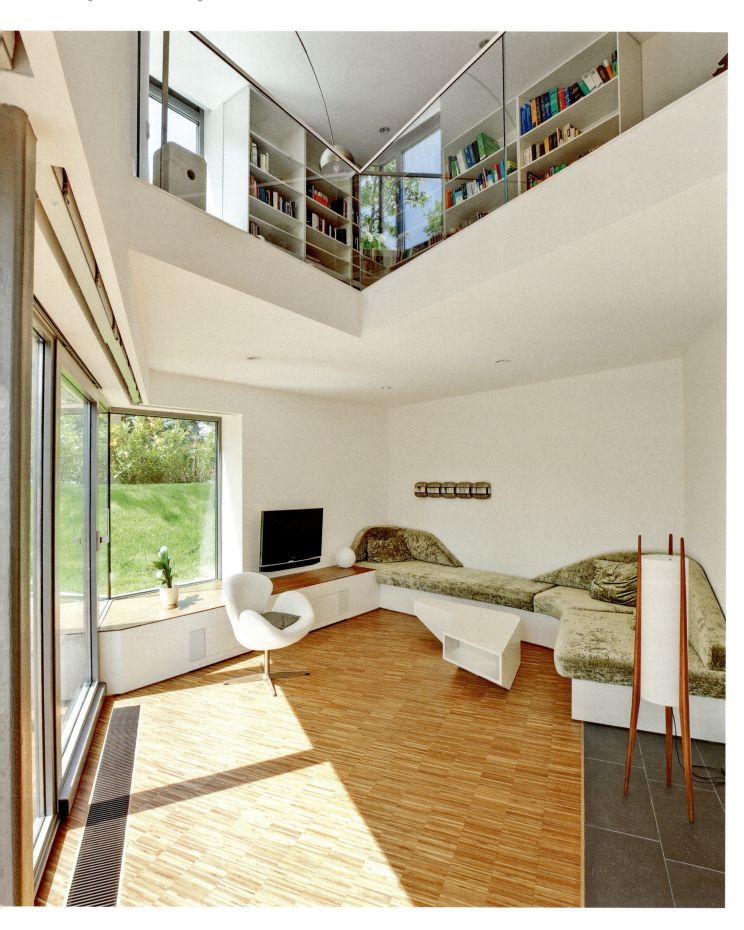

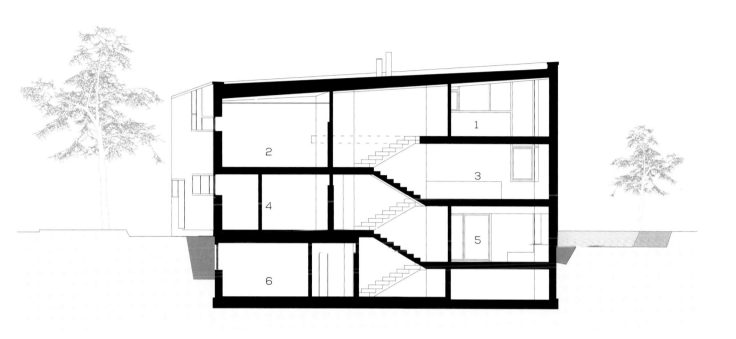

Section

1. Master bedroom
2. Children's room
3. Library - Gallery
4. Kitchen
5. Living room
6. Office

CLIENT | Private client
YEAR | 2009
SIZE | 335m²
STATUS | Built

PROJECT | Multi-family condominium

AO PROJECT
TOKYO | JAPAN

The AO Project, a condominium in Tokyo, is an example of our approach to developing a design from internal and external parameters rather than according to preconceived notions of typology, visual language, or style. The project developed naturally in an evolutionary process, during which GRAFT designed the rules of interaction between specific parameters, rather than the object itself.

The overall appearance of the building is the result of a combination of prescribed urban codes on building setbacks and solar overshadowing, the maximum leasable area, and the iconic image of Japanese mountains. In response to these parameters, GRAFT created a luscious living hill in a dense urban section of Tokyo. The green hill on top of the building spills down the façades and connects the structure to the surrounding streets. The AO Project will therefore change continually with the seasons, an aspect that is highly valued in Japan. The entrance is via a so-called "porte-cochere" that penetrates the building like a tunnel, connecting the street to the main lobby and turning upwards into an atrium to emerge onto the landscaped roof above. This formal device creates a public space that connects all six floors above ground, introducing a dramatic funnel of light into the building.

....

Right | Lobby with crystalline atrium

This spread | Exterior with green roof and façade

The atrium ensures that all residential floors are naturally lit and illuminates the basement floor. From beneath, one has a clear view of the sky from all levels. This play of light continues at night with a constellation of pinpoints of light reflecting off the glass panelling. The motif of a green hill within the almost completely sealed urban environment of Tokyo is additionally informed by sustainability parameters. The atrium brings natural light and air deep into the building, reducing the need for artificial light and mechanical ventilation. A twin-skin glass façade protects it against peak temperatures and, in conjunction with a geothermal system, provides energy-efficient building climate control. Similarly, the green roof is part of the building's water system, collecting and retaining water, and using grey water solutions for irrigation. The roof has its own domestic fauna, and butterflies enjoy the olfactory sensation of rosemary and thyme as much as the residents. This not only serves to cool down the building, but also the immediate urban vicinity.

The formal language of the building shifts progressively from the organic shapes of the public realm and the crystalline atrium to the more private and traditional pattern of rectilinear spaces in Japanese houses.

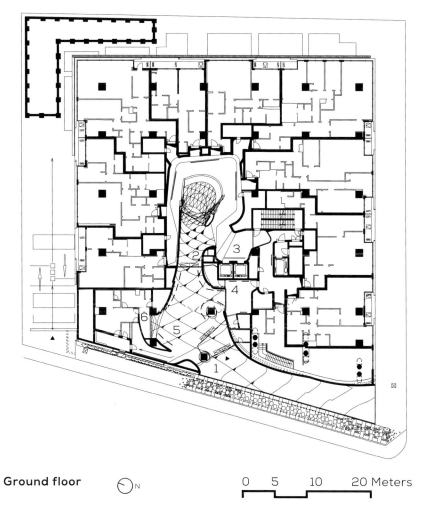

Ground floor   N   0 5 10 20 Meters

1. Main entrance
2. Atrium
3. Corridor
4. Elevator
5. Lobby
6. Reception

This spread | Lobby and first floor

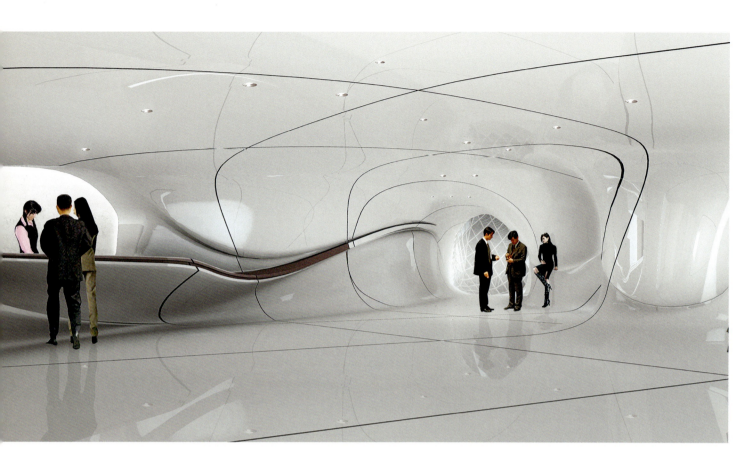

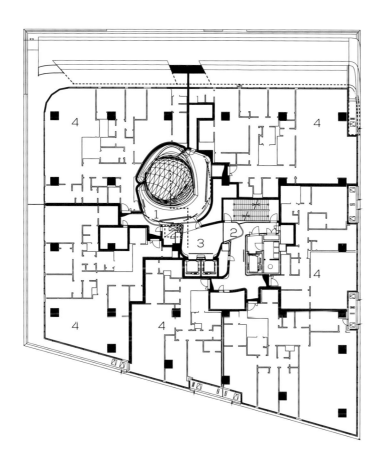

1st floor

1. Atrium
2. Corridor
3. Elevator
4. Apartment spaces

CLIENT | AO Project
YEAR | 2010
SIZE | 15,000m²
STATUS | In progress

PROJECT | Interior design, loft

BEIJING CHATEAU
BEIJING | CHINA

Representative party venue, company guest house and luxury private apartment – these are the varying functions that the showroom for a large-scale development of high-end condominiums needed to fulfill. To this end, GRAFT developed a flexible plan, dominated by a dynamic sculptural element that separates the private rooms from the public reception areas. Semi-transparent spatial dividers, carved in traditional Chinese lattice patterns, can be used to quickly partition off the space for intimate family functions or to open it up for entertaining.

The interior design of a duplex unit in Shoulu Huayan Towers in Beijing, China, as a model apartment for the complex, features a master bedroom on the gallery level and a representative living area and lounge along the façade, ending in a private office. Two guest bedrooms, concealed behind carved semi-transparent doors embedded within a sculptural wall, can be closed off from the remainder of the apartment by folding out the doors, extending the bedrooms up to the façade. The folding doors regulate the degree of privacy and exposure.

In addition to the enclosed Chinese kitchen, the apartment includes a European kitchen with bar counter open to the living area. An open, sculptural stair leads up to the private master bedroom with a terrace and library.

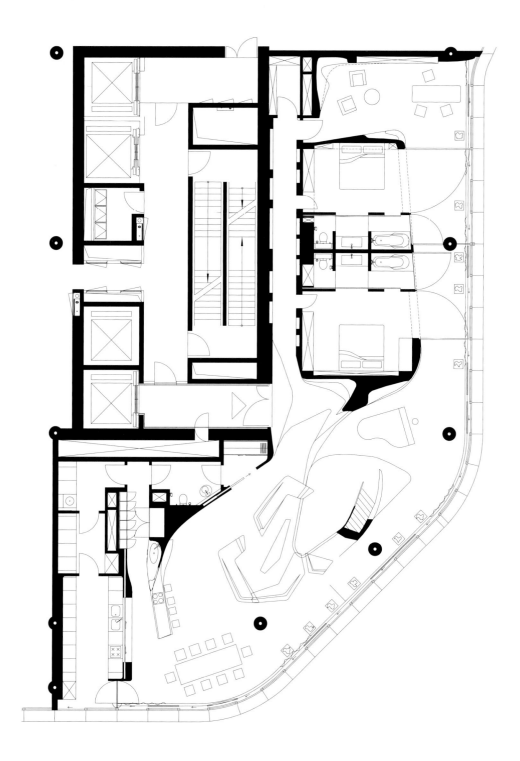

Floor plan

CLIENT | Beijing ShouLu - Hua Yuan Property Co., Ltd.
YEAR | 2005
SIZE | 450m²
STATUS | Built

PROJECT | Masterplanning, residential

FUXIN MIXED USE
BEIJING | CHINA

GRAFT's masterplan for Fuxin in China is located at the border between the old town and a new development area, immediately adjacent to the large-scale residential area of Fuxin-Xiang Yu Yi Pin. The project provides a total gross floor area of 210,000m² above ground and 90,000m² below ground. More than half of the space will be used for mid-level residential and maisonette units of 40m²- 120m², as well as small 45m² studios. Due to its prominent location along Renmin Avenue, the project serves as a landmark feature of the area. In stark contrast to the neighboring projects, the design is conceived as a composition of only three objects: two buildings of extreme length and distinct skyline and a single tower.

One 400m long L-shaped building frames the north and east side, while a second longer building demarcates the south and west side. On the north-west corner this second building bends inward to create a large entrance plaza for the residential complex. It is here that the 82m high freestanding tower stands.
The most prominent aspect of the design is its skyline. Up to 150m long slopes swing up and down along the buildings, creating the visual effect of mountain ranges. The project provides excellent living conditions for up to 2,000 families and adding much needed retail and entertainment facilities for the wider area.

Left | Bird's eye view of Renming Avenue
Right | Street perspective

CLIENT | Fuxin Wanjiaxin Real Estate Development Co., Ltd
YEAR | 2011
SIZE | 300,000m²
STATUS | In progress

PROJECT | Research project "The future of living"

MOONRAKER
BURBANK | USA

What are the future conditions of our daily life? As the paradigm shift in the relationship between living and working becomes increasingly visible, the idea of home is changing. People long for a home as a place to be secure, safe, and well. Traditional functions of rooms will blend, known distinctions between space and furniture will blur, and identity will be created differently with the emergence of the modern-day nomad. Technology will open new territories for how people interact with space and information. Spaces for sanity, meditation, cleansing of the body and the mind will become more and more important. Rooms for contemplation, for peace of the mind, for necessary recharging and self-affirmation will be needed. What will the future private spa look like?

GRAFT designed and built future "Life Settings" as stages of visual communication. Like a set design these interior worlds will be erected within a hangar or loft space as accessible statements, places of experimentation and inspiration. The Moonraker partners will contribute to these efforts with products and consultation.

The future life settings are four built environments representing diverse customer segments that showcase future appropriate technologies, concepts and products in an engaging way. The four futuristic scenarios illustrate a broad spectrum of user types, interests, competencies and aesthetics. The installation can be modified to suit a variety of foreseeable scenarios and uses.

CLIENT | Volkswagen America / Moonraker Group
YEAR | 2006
SIZE | 1,100m²
STATUS | Built

PROJECT | Product design, lighting
CLIENT | Zumtobel Lighting GmbH
IN COLLABORATION WITH | Felix Götze

CAELA LIGHTING SYSTEM

The CAELA LED luminaire range turns the lighting system into a design item: in close cooperation with GRAFT, Zumtobel has developed a decorative luminaire that combines elegance and lightness.

Thanks to maximum efficiency and innovative light distribution, the luminaire range is suited to solve a vast variety of lighting tasks.

The CAELA LED luminaire range uses an innovative, flat design and two different types of light distribution. As a wall-mounted, ceiling-mounted and pendant luminaire, CAELA appears extremely slim and elegant, with a maximum depth of 55 mm. CAELA is available as a round or square luminaire with a diameter or side length of 330mm and 430mm and in white, matt silver, copper, brass, matt grey and black. There are switchable and dimmable models, with a luminous flux of 1,000 and 1,500lm.

In addition to symmetrical standard light distribution, the square version of the wall-mounted luminaire also features innovative asymmetrical light distribution specifically developed to meet the lighting requirements in corridors and staircases, where the light is precisely directed onto the walls and floors.

PROJECT | Product design
CLIENT | Franz Schneider Brakel GmbH + Co KG

FSB 1246

GRAFT designed a new family of door handles for the manufacturer FSB.

FSB 1246 unites modern simplicity with ergonomic handling. Its narrow radii but broad sweep create sculptural tension and contrast, lending the minimal form a compelling aesthetic quality. The durable cylindrical handles are well-proportioned, offering users a comfortable grip. Its clean lines make it suitable for a wide range of architectural contexts.

The FSB 1246 product family encompasses glass door fittings, frame door handles, door knobs and window handles. They are manufactured from aluminum and are available with a polished or a natural color anodized surface finish.

PROJECT | Product design, furniture
CLIENT | ipdesign

FAT TONY

FAT TONY is a modular seating system with a highly flexible "kit of parts" that allows for a huge spectrum of variation possibilities.

GRAFT designed it as three flexible cubic modules, making it uniquely versatile and suitable for many different scenarios. The sofa can be altered according to different everyday requirements and room configurations thanks to easily moveable elements: FAT TONY can be used as a sofa system, couch, armchair, chaise longue or stool. An unusual upholstery structure creates a special, ergonomic feeling. Instead of sinking in, you are supported in an ideal sitting position. FAT TONY's zigzag and coil springs are longer-lasting and more comfortable than a simple foam block, thus guaranteeing maximum quality. The high-grade upholstery in the back and base ensures maximum comfort, and solid beech load-bearing parts keep the modules in shape for a whole lifetime.

The free choice of textile furnishings allows for complete individualization. FAT TONY configurations are available in single colors as well as completely multi-colored. The elements can be detached and put together without much work, so that the whole combination can be re-arranged according to different needs.

PROJECT | Product design, furniture
CLIENT | ipdesign

DRIFT INTERPROFIL LOUNGE

The "Drift" lounger is the static moment of an object in motion. Its dynamic contours express a balance between a state of rest and movement. By "drifting", the three separate entities can form different functional configurations. Oscillating between a "bed continent", a continuous "horse shoe" and an "ensemble of freestanding objects", "Drift" can fulfill almost all lounging desires.

Its design reflects what we need most in a modern world: calmness in motion. "Drift" invites the restless to come back home – here one can truly enjoy calmness while everything else is in motion.

PROJECT | Product design
CLIENT | Kanera GmbH & Co. KG

KANERA SINK

Ever since the late 19th century – in other words ever since private bathrooms have existed – washbasins have tended to be wall-mounted or positioned next to a wall. Now the washbasin can be moved to the center of the bathroom. In this respect, the KANERA 1 D double washbasin presents a revolutionary spatial concept: for the first time, a double washbasin has been designed as a standalone installation within the bathroom. It not only offers the shared experience of the poetry of water, but also enables completely new room layouts.
It makes an inspiring statement, and in doing so sets the stage for architects and designers to develop new bathroom interiors that reflect their clients' wishes, freeing up the positioning of bathtub, shower, washstand solutions and furniture modules and making it possible to orchestrate the experience of water as an element.

The 1.6 × 1.2m KANERA 1 D is compatible with a wide range of base furniture units, and the range of options for the configuration of the washbasin, materials and functions is almost limitless. GRAFT's design for the double washbasin made of enamelled steel creates a "washing place" that can form the heart of a room, turning the bathroom into a haven, a reflection of the owner's personality, while simultaneously exerting a powerful fascination as an art object.

This spread | Kanera 1D

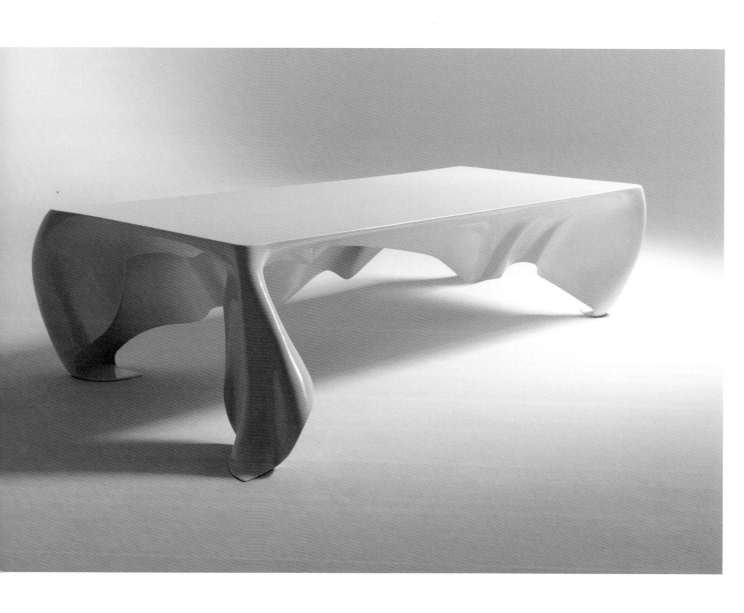

PROJECT | Product design
CLIENT | Stilwerk

PHANTOM TABLE

A table has always been something special. We spend many of our most important moments at or around it. We take care of basic needs such as satisfying our hunger and quenching our thirst, and sometimes more sublime, celebrate fine dining and good wine. We make important decisions, we invent the future and celebrate being in the moment. But the essence, the really important aspect of a table, is that it brings us together. Therefore, the table deserves a special place in our home, and in our lives. For this reason we were interested in designing a table, and with it, be able to search for those collectively creative moments.

In 1955, when the most famous dress in the history of films reversed gravity with the support of a floor ventilator, it simultaneously exposed the beautiful legs of Marilyn Monroe. We remember this sensual moment filled with lightness, playfulness and humor. An iconic picture icon of the 20th century was created, an important milestone in the gradual flow of life. We seek these magical moments in our work, because they define our lives and make it worth living for: when unsurpassed laughter frees us of conventions, or the birth of an idea saves the world. Talking, eating and drinking at the table can shut out a crazy world for a few magical moments together.

The table designed by GRAFT captures a similar moment. As the table cloth starts to sway, seemingly gathering momentum by the energy of the beseated, and is about to take off, it reveals... that there is no table underneath. As if it never existed. A phantom. A moment of movement that leads to revelation: not the table is important, but much rather the people sitting around it!

PROJECT | Product design, furniture

BIBLIOLONGUE

Transitional fossils are evolutionary biological organisms featuring characteristics of two groups of living beings. However, they are not directly related to these two groups, and may just be close relatives. Transitional fossils are an intermediary or transitional form, organisms that unite characteristics of phylogenetically older and younger biological groups.

Looking at the Bibliolongue from an evolutionary point of view, it appears suspended between the principles of an orthogonal and a free form vocabulary. This creative hubris results in a surprising and sensible experience.

The outer perimeter of the lounge is made of stained multiplex board, miter-joined at the corners. The surface of the seating area is milled into the wood and follows the contours of the body, creating an ergonomic seat that is further emphasized by the horizontality of the multiplex boards.

The creative hubris of the Bibliolongue is expressed by is functional ambiguity. It is at once a repository for the reader to store his or her beloved books and a place to read them. As such, it embodies the principle of GRAFT, creating a Bibliolongue through the grafting of a "bibliothèque" with a "chaise longue".

RESIDENTIAL PROJECTS
WORLDWIDE

BIRDS ISLAND ›› p.44
BEIJING CHATEAU ›› p.214
MOONRAKER ›› p.222
VECAKI-VILLA

PITT STUDIO ›› p.60
ZEAL
LOFT GLEIMSTRASSE ›› p.136

ALEXANDER TOWER
PANORAMA TOWERS ›› p.76
AO-DI NEXT GENE VILLA

ESIDE VILLA >> p.100
E IT RIGHT >> p.152
S KOCH >> p.200

GENERATION SILVER 65+
HAUSVOGTEIPLATZ
AO PROJECT >> p.206
LOFT HAMBURG >> p.122

GARDEN STUDIO
IBA HAMBURG
MAKE IT RIGHT NEWARK

RESIDENTIAL PROJECTS
WORLDWIDE

HAUS BERG
FUXIN MIXED USE ›› p.218
VILLA SIXT
FALKENRIED

CBD BEIJING ›› p. 22
ORDOS 20+10
ALMSTADTSTRASSE ›› p.114

LOFT HAUSVOGTEIPLATZ ›› p.86
HAUS HARDER
KRONPRINZENGÄRTEN

:HLERTSTRASSE
A VIENNA >> p.52
L FRIEDRICHSTRASSE

HINES APARTMENTS
VILLA STÖLPCHENSEE
LUXE LAKE RESIDENTIAL TOWER

ENTENWERDER
HH BAAKENHAFEN
TOR149 >> p.66

RESIDENTIAL PROJECTS
WORLDWIDE

MINISTERGÄRTEN
YANTAI URBAN DEVELOPMENT
FORT PECK

TELTOWN >> p.168
AFFORDABLE HOUSING NAMIBIA >> p.160

AUENFLÜGEL >> p.192
HOLISTIC LIVING >> p.26
VILLA J >> p.130

ZOWUFER
AGON APARTMENTS ›› p.10
WERK ›› p.36

HEIMAT2 ›› p.146
WAVE ›› p.108
CHARLIE LIVING ›› p.182
VILLA M ›› p.96

BLÜTENVIERTEL ›› p.188
BRICKS ›› p.172
TEMPLINER STRASSE ›› p.80

NEW WAYS OF DWELLING

THE RELEVANCE OF THE FLOOR PLAN.
FORM FOLLOWS THE ARCHITECT'S TOOLS.

The revolutionary development of form-finding tools in 3D computer-aided design systems over the past 25 years has radically transformed the design process and the education of architects. Today, parametric design software and BIM models have become the tools of choice, making it possible to intelligently optimize interdependent architectural parameters such as structure, use, sustainability and health. Architects can now design increasingly complex and aesthetically daring forms while keeping track of their implications on other functional and architectural aspects. These new tools have helped architects venture into uncharted territories and have the potential to change the profession on a historic scale. In the current debate within the architectural discipline on methodologies, digital aesthetics and the "right way forward" in general, GRAFT favors what they call "Toolbox Total", using the possibilities offered by a new set of tools to enhance traditional knowledge and skills with a view to expanding horizons and improving architecture as a whole.

In this exploratory age, the relevance of the floor plan, the 2D representation of layout as a generator of form, seems to be waning to the extent that it is increasingly becoming almost a by-product of the 3D design process. The plan is no longer the driver of form and the days in which Le Corbusier or Frank Lloyd Wright proclaimed that everything follows from the floor plan are long gone.

At the same time 2D plans are still the most common means of communicating architectural designs, both to clients and between planners, consultants and construction firms. While we already communicate form using 3D models and photorealistic perspectives, floor plans are still the favored form for communicating the actual function of architecture and calculating its economic basis. The program of spaces, area schedule and especially the designation of the "use" of a space, be it a residential or an office environment, a private or a communal area, define everything that can be quantified and measured, the means of access and grades of accessibility, as well as fire escape routes, material quality, lighting aspects, and so on. Defining "uses" in area schedules can also have tax implications for the owners and users. It is 2D plans rather than 3D models that serve as legal documents, and area calculations that serve as the basis for deriving the financial realities of each project.

....

Left | GRAFT's plus-energy houses combine the aspects of mobility, energy and health with smart floor plans

....

When it comes to describing "use", we are bound to a vocabulary of legal terms and a common understanding of what the functions of a building will (presumably) be. So it is not surprising that while the way we live our lives may have changed dramatically, we are still used to seeing typical labels such as "living room", "dining room", "office", "bedroom", "lobby", "hallway", etc. in floor plans. Such terms – simplified descriptions of use – seem to be the common vocabulary of all residential design, no matter what style or philosophy. But do we really still live according to these categories? Can such simplifications reflect the variety of lifestyles and individual personalities of those living in the buildings we design? Can they adequately respond to the growing diversity of living cultures that only rarely match the lifestyle categories defined by developers and bankers, investors and lawyers?

It seems that the simpler our definition of architectural function, the more arbitrary the relationship between the function and its form. At the same time, the more we try and accurately describe functions, the more we open them up to unpredictable ways of use. Does this mean by implication that the more banal our description of function, the more banal the building will be, the more moderate its functional interpretation, the more mediocre the end result?

The reality is that our ways of life as well as our consumption patterns are changing rapidly: many of us are already used to working at home, at the kitchen table or even in bed, on the train and in public areas with public wi-fi, maybe even in a park or at the poolside. Similarly, we have grown used to eating in the car, while walking or in front of the TV. Through Airbnb and other digital social networks, we are increasingly opening our most private spaces to the world. All these changes in our daily routines affect the way we experience and use our built environment. They determine how we use our personal space. At GRAFT we think that the conventional definitions of "functions" of architecture need to be questioned and adapted in response to a cultural shift in priorities and behavior.

But how can we take into account individual ways of living, unpredictable changes in routines and the behavior of very different inhabitants over the life cycle of a building? How can architecture accommodate the need to adapt to new habits or changing needs?

What if we were to begin from the assumption that programmatic scenarios are likely to be contradicting and complementary? Instead of concentrating on designing for functions, architecture would offer spatial qualities – the beauty of form – that can be a setting for different and changing scenographies – the beauty of function. Buildings need to have a strong identity and offer great interactive flexibility: architecture needs to define form in a way that enables the customization of function.

If we consider Louis Sullivan's now 150-year-old seminal credo of "form follows function", it is astonishing how much form has diversified while the vocabulary of function has pretty much remained the same. Many authors have since replaced "function" in Louis Sullivan's famous saying with "fiction", "fashion", "emotion", "nature", or another term, usually to justify a formal debate. But perhaps it is not the replacement term but the difficulty we have in agreeing on what "use" or "function" is that offers a key to the problem. Maybe it is even the quality of the term "use" that it can stand for many things, that it offers a richness that provides room for interpretation and uniqueness in architecture? But to rediscover the potential of "dynamic use", we need to take a closer look at the floor plan and rediscover the virtuosity of this dormant tool of architectural design.

....

By assuming contradicting and complimentary programmatic settings, architecture can provide both:

spatial quality (the beauty of the form) and a stage setting for very different and changing scenographies (beauty of the function).

....

The more unconventional and experimental we tried to be in making our buildings and spaces usable in different ways, the more exciting and interesting the discussion about its form became. It started with a bath tub next to the bed in the middle of a hotel room, with a desert room filled with sand in the center of a spa (both in Hotel Q!, Berlin) and with early studies on using the ceiling in a restaurant to define degrees of intimacy (Fix Restaurant, Las Vegas). In an early residential project, we took the bold step of making an apartment flexible enough to be a series of small, private spaces or an open plan area for parties and receptions. To this end, we superimposed Adolf Loos' "Raumplan" on Le Corbusier's "plan libre" in one and the same apartment in Berlin's Prenzlauer Berg district. Large-format sliding walls allow the residents to either subdivide or completely do away with the inner logic of separate rooms. It was the owner, completely taken by the idea of the mix of functions, who finally insisted on having a bath tub built into the sofa cocoons in a space formerly known as the "living room". In a loft apartment in Hamburg, we explored a variation of the same programmatic idea, making it possible for the residents to convert the entire space to any needed use. By visually opening up a diagonal line through the apartment, the sense of volume becomes spacious and expansive.

This playful approach to the layout of floor plans is not limited to larger apartments, and becomes even more interesting when applied to smaller spaces. The "Paragon Apartment" (Paragon-greek for example) is a 37.5m² mini-loft that was developed by GRAFT to make an inner-city apartment as small as possible, and therefore affordable, while making it comfortable and flexible at the same time. The key is the wet area with two entrance doors and a sliding wall separating the sleeping area (private studiolo) from the rest of the apartment. This central, cabinet-like element allows space to flow continuously around it: views always lead on or around instead of ending at the corner of the "room". This floor plan has since been modified and developed for two additional apartment buildings in Berlin, currently under construction.

The need for simplicity paired with flexibility at the smallest residential scale is taken to the next level in a project for the KfW (Kreditanstalt für Wiederaufbau) aimed at providing affordable housing concepts for Namibia. To make it possible for people to acquire property, and thereby invest in their habitat, GRAFT developed the idea of a minimal core house that combines the wet areas, kitchen and bath with a stair leading up to a bedroom on the second level. This 16m² structural core can be prefabricated, and serves as a basis for further simple additions and extensions. The key to this project is the simplicity and affordability of the core, and the possibility to extend it in all directions, in multiple different ways and formal expressions.

———

The Paragon apartment

Developed in 2013, this apartment has served as the basis for numerous variations in subsequent GRAFT projects, often in combination with communal areas in larger apartment projects. Its basis is a 37.5m² space with full-height glazing and balcony along one side offering a panoramic view. The size is optimized to be a compact two-room apartment with a separate "bedroom" for sleeping that can nevertheless be joined to the main space with kitchen and flexible living area by retracting a sliding partition. Both spaces then benefit from the full window frontage.

The bathroom has two doors – one from the entrance area and one from the bedroom – avoiding the need for corridors and allowing circular movement through the apartment, making it feel bigger than it is.

This apartment type works well in large apartment buildings and in combination with generous communal or club areas on the ground floor or on the roof as seen, for example, in the Paragon and Charlie Living projects. The small size makes living in highly attractive urban areas more affordable.

>> See page 10

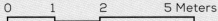

0 1 2 5 Meters

Left | The rooftop "Loft Gleimstrasse" unites all functions into a continuous and highly flexible open floor plan

Loft Gleimstrasse

A C-shaped rooftop of a typical Berlin apartment building became the subject of a spatial experiment to unite two contradicting spatial concepts: Le Corbusier's "plan libre" and Adolf Loos' "Raumplan". A central sculpture wrapped in a curvilinear skin of inclined walls contains the stair core, storage cabinets, private bathrooms and sauna and is the element that integrates all areas of the continuous plan. The kitchen and a large table occupy the bottleneck between the front and the back of the apartment, marking the center of the longest corridor of view. Six large sliding walls make it possible to subdivide the open space in diverse constellations. Bedrooms, guest areas and bathrooms can be separated off from the open space. The front and back façades can be opened completely, blurring the boundary between indoors and outdoors. The result is a highly flexible grafting of the ideas of "Raumplan" and "plan libre".

›› See page 136

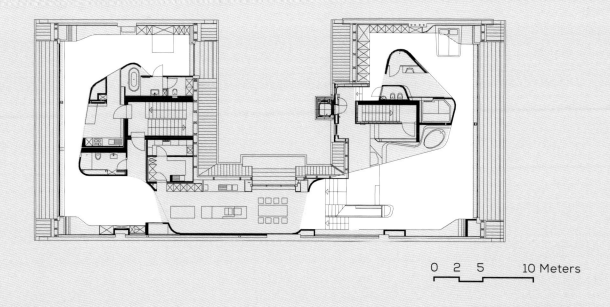

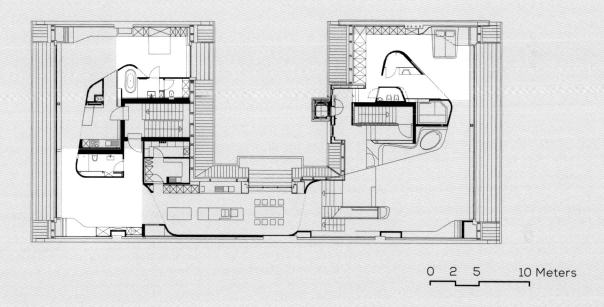

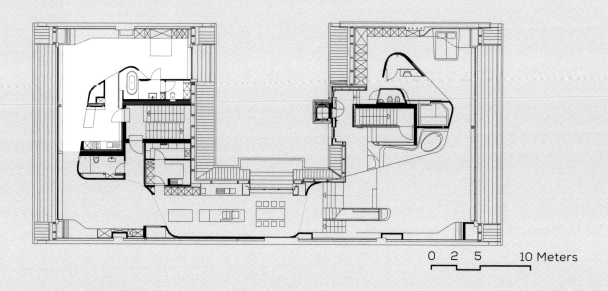

It should be easy to inhabit a space, but more so to adjust it to changing needs and moods.

THE IDEAL HOME.
MULTIPLE FUNCTIONS, MULTIPLE READINGS.

———

For us "perceiving beauty" and "affording accessibility" are equally important "functions" of architecture. Likewise enabling "forms of representation", creating opportunities for "privacy", for "communicating", "inspiration", "dreaming", or "freeing up the mind" are also some of the most relevant "functions" of the built environment.

The ideal of a home in our view is liberating and exciting. Home should be an environment that we dream of and a space that inspires us. As the way we live together and the notion of home are constantly changing, new residential architecture should always be a "proof of concept" that communicates and celebrates the complexity of our lives.

At GRAFT we love building flexibility into our designs. It should be easy to inhabit a space, and also just as easy to adjust it to changing needs and moods. Residential design does not have to reflect one single idea of how to live but should challenge and support the imagination of its inhabitants. Private living spaces should be adaptable settings and environments for rest, inspiration, stimulation and social interaction. They must cater for a fundamental need for shelter and intimacy and also be places for representative moments of hospitality and conviviality.

We as architects do not want to define everything through our design, but instead to challenge and enable. Looking back at our residential projects, we have never been in favor of one particular way of sculpting space. We don't believe cultural and behavioral trends are easily predictable, but we generally assume that most of our "clients" will want to inhabit a playful environment that is easily accessible and can be adapted according to personal wishes.

In the end our goal is to understand form as an expression of a pluralistic culture of individuals who, in larger entities can reinvent the idea of communities. At the heart of any project is a particular idea of openness and flexibility.

While we too participate in the discussion on "function" and "use", we prefer to call it "scenography" or the "stage setting" of architecture as a way of reflecting and expressing contemporary ways of living. Given the scant attention paid to function in the ongoing debates on form over the past 150 years, one could conclude that in many cases form follows anything but function!

Considering "function" in more complex terms as something dynamic, hybrid, flexible and individual effects a shift away from fixed, repetitive and ultimately banal design solutions, opening up possibilities for variation, complexity and more daring designs – not just in niche luxury design markets but also in projects for affordable living spaces.

———

Loft Hamburg

At first sight, this apartment is an open mini-loft with a central core. What makes this small space unique is how it makes the most of the longest distance in the space by celebrating the diagonal view. The position of the bed has the best view and is also the point de vue.

The spatial concept combines a hotel room type with en-suite bathroom on one side (A) with a more formal gathering space with open kitchen (B) on the other side of the central core. The open plan allows both areas to flow into each other but they can be separated with two large sliding walls (C) into two to create a formal and an intimate area.

The central core houses all the wet areas: kitchen and bathroom, visually connected by a horizontal window. The bath tub is part of the perimeter wall of the main space but visually connected when seen from the bathing area. Sofa cocoons allow the perimeter walls to be inhabited and a built-in sideboard can be transformed into a work desk. Architectural form and furniture blend into one.

›› See page 122

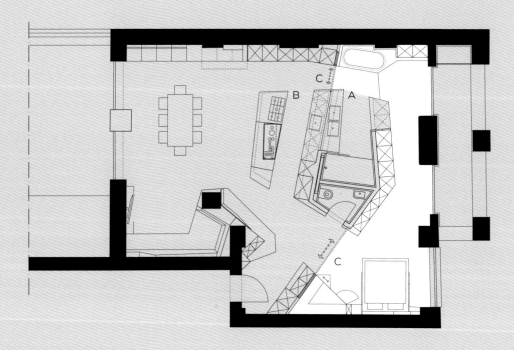

The flexible floor plan and large slidings doors of "Loft Hamburg" allow for an open loft space...

... or seperated formal and intimate areas

Plus-energy Houses Holistic Living

GRAFT's design for a single-family house and two semidetached houses combines the aspects of mobility, energy and healthy living with environmentally-friendly construction. Aside from the use of innovative technology, and healthy and eco-friendly materials and construction methods, all houses combine two different spatial concepts in their floor plans: Rectangular sleeping rooms, offering panoramic views, are arranged on the second floor whereas the ground floor celebrates the freedom of an open floor plan around a central stair core and fire place. Large floor-to-ceiling windows and sliding doors connect indoor and outdoor spaces, creating a sense of seamless flow in this large open, communal area. The design concept for the house evolves as a „grafting" of two formal layouts on top of each other.

›› See page 26

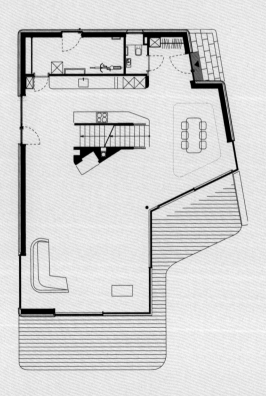
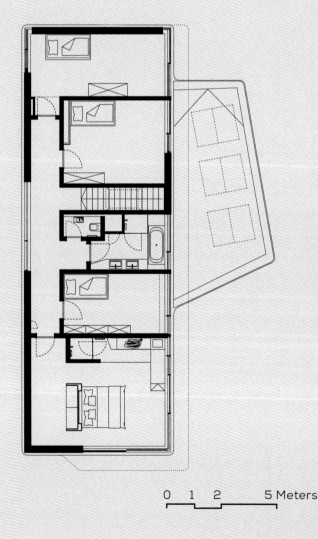

GRAFT Berlin II Apartment

GRAFT designed a 90m² two-bedroom apartment for a residential building at Teutoburger Platz (Berlin, Prenzlauer Berg) that includes a walk-in-closet, a guest toilet and a utility room, program components usually only expected from much larger residential spaces. Its layout shows a bathroom "core" in the center as a combination of guest toilet and bathroom dividable by a sliding door. Those two combined form a bath of decent size with two basins, shower and bathtub. A corridor from the main living areas to the main bedroom serves as walk-in closet and bathroom vestibule. Instead of a second toilet the apartment has a utility room. The resulting circular route through the apartment allows for long views through the entire space of the apartment.

>> See page 80

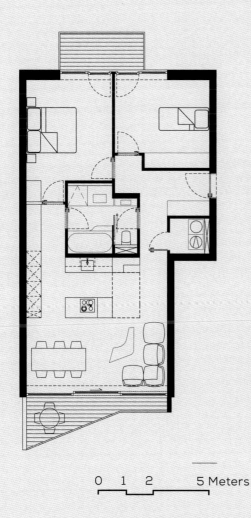

0 1 2   5 Meters

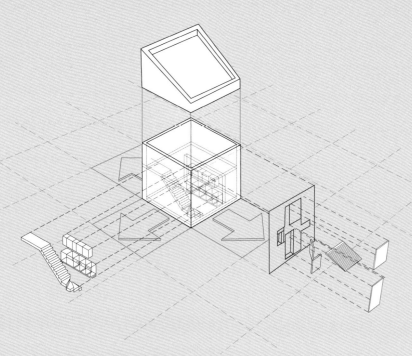

Affordable Housing Namibia

Namibia is experiencing a housing crisis with half a million people living in unsafe shack settlements. The average prices for houses and apartments have become unaffordable for over 90% of the population. The shortage of housing for low-income households is a serious social problem and is considered an impediment to development in the country, with an increasing backlog currently estimated at over 75,000 houses. For individuals, ownership also means obtaining an asset that can be used as collateral for future bank loans and thus further financial and social security. The severe shortage of housing units was the starting point for a feasibility study by GRAFT, commissioned by the KfW development bank on behalf of the Development Bank of Namibia (DBN).

The study aims to demonstrate the viability of creating 1,000 efficient affordable housing units on the private market. GRAFT developed the idea of a prefabricated 16m² core house that combines the wet areas, kitchen and bath with a stair leading up to a bedroom on the second level. It is not a final product but a starter kit for those looking to get going with the smallest initial investment while still having the potential to extend later according to changing needs and financial possibilities. The modularity of the core is echoed by a modular façade system made of standardized key components that can be combined in different ways. It is the basis for further additions and extensions and can also accommodate mixed-use functions: the street frontage of all the house units can be used as a built-in sales area for businesses of different scales.

›› See page 160

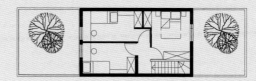

Small townhouse | Core S

Small townhouse | Core M1

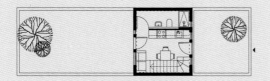
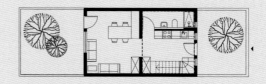

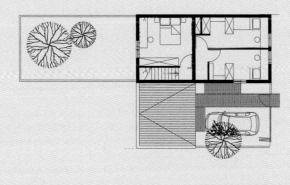
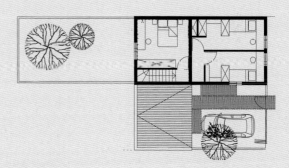

Courtyard house | Core B1

Courtyard house | Core B2

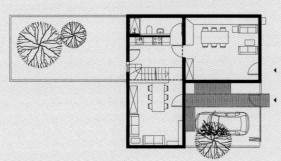
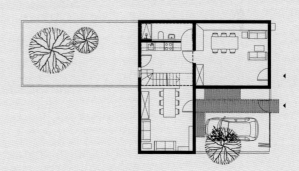

STORIES ARE THE SOCIAL CURRENCY OF THE WORLD

THE ULTRA-LOCAL

Hotels and residential buildings are two architectural typologies that cater to very similar fundamental human needs, on the one hand providing shelter and privacy and on the other acting as stages for social interaction. As boundaries between the private and public blur, we are seeing a transformation of residential typologies. But have apartment buildings been learning from hotels? Or is it the other way around, as the "home away from home" slogans of hotels around the world would have us believe?

While hotels still seek to provide a sense of home, they have had to acknowledge the fact that customers are increasingly rejecting the idea of generic, repetitive design, as seen in large hotel chains in favor of a true authentic and local experience. The sharing economy, with platforms like airbnb and couchsurfing, has boosted this trend even further, merging the residential and hospitality sector into a new contemporary travel market. Now actual homes are the new hotels.

Consequently, it is not surprising that hotels have begun recalibrating their services, offering their own exclusive branded apartments linked to hotels. Similarly, apartment building concepts now come with a broad variety of "communal add-ons" such as community spaces, club rooms, communal gardens, even room service, cleaning, mail delivery, childcare facilities and kindergarten. Self-organized collectives in which families and individuals co-finance and develop their own dwellings are a further example of new trends and micro-experiments that are just getting off the ground. The digital revolution of our means and tools of social interaction and communication is influencing new processes in the much slower discipline of architecture and urban development. We are growing accustomed to new ways of interacting, cooperating and organizing ourselves, sharing our experiences even across large distances in real time. In times of growing physical and psychological mobility, we expect our environments to be reactive and to enable diverse ways of living and travelling instead of dictating how we are supposed to behave.

To appeal to these new target groups, many hotels are busily shedding their image of a formal and disciplined environment and instead presenting a more welcoming and playful stage, emphasizing easy access and local anchors. Exclusivity and accessibility are no longer a contradiction. Hotels can be representative and informal at the same time. When we look at the boom in boutique hotels and the rise of diversified brands like the "Design Hotels" group, we see a successful combination of casual and luxurious design, of openness and privacy. In this respect, hotels can still be prototypes of new living concepts.

…………

Left | The concept of re-contextualization for the "Old Mill Hotel" in Belgrade fuses local heritage and contemporary interior design into a single whole

....

By extension, we at GRAFT believe that we are going to see more innovative use concepts, maybe even buildings with no fixed "use" that can be transformed or customized according to contemporary needs. Will the increasing overlap of the realms of work, private living and travel lead to a wholesale change in the legal basis for architecture and urban planning by erasing the fundamental 20th century credo of functional separation? One thing is for sure: redefining the programmatic parameters of hotels will redefine the building typology itself.

We are observing a shift in the travel sector away from mainstream luxury concepts towards more specialized, curated experiences. New patterns of travel are emerging as today's consumers look beyond the classic luxury icons in search of a more individualized, authentic journey. Travel and hotel experiences are being designed around specific lifestyle concepts, such as communal learning, responsible living, and ecological principles, addressing an emotional depth that can often only be offered within a highly localized context. The architecture addressing such new traveller profiles needs to follow a locally anchored narrative.

Stories are the social currency of the world and narratives want to be read, told, understood and interpreted. Stories and their narration have always been an important part of human culture. They act as guard rails for social contracts and moral behavior, and serve as tools to embed and access knowledge, truth, and memory. Architecture based on a narrative scenography follows a long tradition of opening and enabling spaces rather than creating finished products with which the owner, resident or user then merely interacts, perhaps making the odd modification or addition.

For the successful design of any hospitality development, a key aspect is tapping into the spirit of the place, its genius loci, as a means of revealing unique stories and unfolding a distinctive spatial and emotional experience. Taking this "gift of the land" as a starting point, we have the fascinating opportunity to establish new milestones in destination building in a fast-changing tourism market. By listening to what the topography suggests, by enhancing its specific qualities or contrasting them with a new concept, architects can create new and interesting hybrid destinations.

A project's architectural language can draw inspiration from the local vernacular, making use of local materials and respecting the uniqueness of the site. Why create something new, where there is real value to be found everywhere in local contours, flavors, traditions and narratives, all of which contribute to a character that can be enhanced, contrasted, blended or fused with other design ideas that are inherently part of devising a new hospitality experience and that have to meet international expectations, demands and technological standards. We are beginning to see the emergence of a new kind of architecture that is both local and different, sustainable and dynamic, building and landscape, exhilaratingly new and yet rooted in an environment. The trick lies in successfully grafting the existing and the new into a new aesthetic experience where we can relax and learn, discovering sides of ourselves we did not know we have. Sometimes local conditions on site may at first seem like an obstacle, but they have huge potential to anchor a project.

A hotel is a "home" for a fixed duration. It allows us as guests to experiment with conceptual structures, architectures and rituals that we would not usually try at home. We can engage with people, expand our personal horizons and follow learning curves that we cannot easily access in our daily lives. For architects, it is a wonderful opportunity to be able to invent these curated experiences. A hotel is in fact a laboratory of living. We accept that we will be challenged, and hope to discover something new in ourselves through new spatial configurations that allow us to experiment with how we dwell.

Designing the entire customer experience and not just the architecture is the key to developing a holistic product or concept for an aspiring hospitality project. The experience begins within the idea of a place, long before the actual trip happens, unravels with the sequence of arrival and ends with tangible experiences that create memories that continue to resonate long after the guest is back home.

———

"Beauty:
the adjustment of all parts proportionately so that one cannot add or subtract or change without impairing the harmony of the whole"

Leon Battista Alberti
De re aedificatoria (1452)

"There are no passengers on spaceship earth. We are all crew."

Marshall McLuhan

COMMUNITY COMMUTERS

———

In the same way that we believe hotels can celebrate living experiments and test progressive ways of dwelling in the future, we are convinced that hotels are ideal vehicles for testing and implementing new and innovative concepts of sustainability and circular economies.

Together with our experienced network of engineers and consultants we have realised multiple international projects that meet LEED, BREEAM or DGNB standards. It is our goal to create sustainable projects for the service-oriented and internationally connected community without harming natural resources, whether locally or further afield. In all our projects we incorporate our tried and tested "lean-mean-green" strategy and "cradle-to-cradle" thinking. It is important to take into account sustainable development criteria from an early stage in a project, beginning with a nature-sensitive, low-impact strategy for the placement of buildings and infrastructure. It reduces impact on the environment, increases consumer satisfaction, leads to lower life cycle costs and a higher real estate value, to mention just a few advantages.

The faster the world around us appears to accelerate and our relationship to place erodes through our increased exposure to the endless boundaries of the digital realm, the more we seek to anchor our experiences in the strength and unity of community, whether at home or when we travel. The term authenticity is already aging quickly, as it is often just a simulated local reality of a copied identity. At GRAFT, we try and engage with what we call the ultra-local, the quality that truthfully anchors a built destination into its local culture, vernacular and people. This approach not only encompasses local artisanship, building materials and techniques, but also seeks to interact with local communities, for example in the production of food, but also knowledge and craftsmanship in the building of the new destination.

Community is formed not only through encounters at the poolside and in the restaurant, but also through a journey of engaging serendipities and discoveries throughout the destination. The rediscovery of a slow originality, sidelined in recent decades in the global race for everything-now-everywhere, can be transcended into true experiences and new aesthetic adventures, thereby creating something absolutely unique and new: a real community for a certain time and place.

———

Stack Restaurant

In the case of the Stack restaurant in Las Vegas, the image of the great canyons of America's Southwest not only makes reference to the surroundings of the hallucinating desert city, but also manages to resolve the problem of the floor plan's bottleneck.

›› See page 400

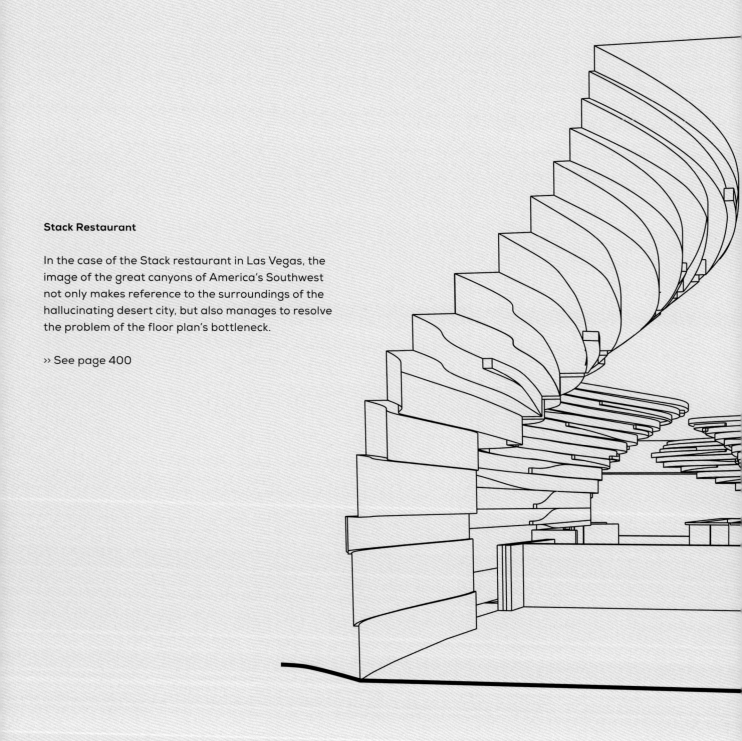

This spread | Line drawing of canyon inspired wall structure

Water Cay

The above-water pavilion for a resort in the Caribbean was informed by natural images that blend the flight of birds with the sweep of the manta ray, translating the location's fauna into the form of the building while at the same time addressing the need for shade and cross-ventilation.

›› See page 480

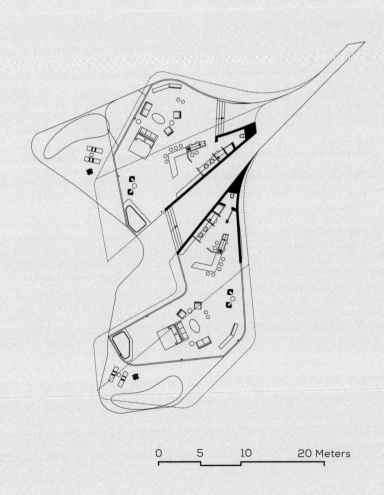

0 5 10 20 Meters

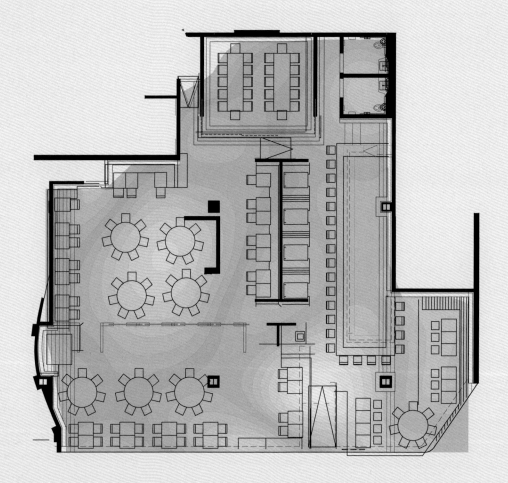

FIX

In the Fix Restaurant inside Bellagio Casino in Las Vegas, the topography of the ceiling reflects the intimacy or openness we wanted to create for each particular table in the layout of the floor plan: the ceiling soars above large tables, and descends towards the edges to create more private conditions at the space's perimeter. This undulating sound reflector also creates an acoustic landscape of louder areas in the center and calmer areas at the surrounding rendezvous tables.
The ceiling also incorporates technical equipment – smoke detectors, speakers and air outlets – but the ceiling's dominant logic is oriented around creating a landscape of privacy. In this respect, the architecture reflects and supports the simple human ritual of collective dining.

›› See page 412

Gingko Restaurant

The design of the Gingko Bacchus restaurant in Chengdu, China employs several visual techniques to showcase and reveal the overall storyline of the project: the Greek god Bacchus and the appreciation of food and wine.

In the entrance area, large format photographs by the Australian artist Kevin Best depict luscious still-life scenes inspired by Baroque paintings on the wall behind the reception desk. The images are placed behind one-way mirrors and equipped with a time-controlled backlighting system. Certain aspects of the images emerge and fade over time, steeping the entire hallway in slow motion. As the light fades, the image disappears, and the beholder is then reflected in the one-way mirror.

Each private dining room in the Ginkgo Bacchus has its own custom wallpaper of staple food produce, such as carrots, mushrooms, walnuts, broccoli, beans, chilies, and artichokes. In each of the nine rooms one wall features a famous painting of Bacchus, laser-cut as a pixelated abstraction into stainless steel panels. Through the laser-cut pixels of the historical Bacchus paintings, visitors can see the illuminated background of the vegetable wallpaper and Arcadian landscapes. The experience unfolds through moments of revelation, concealment and mental projection.

›› See page 424

Old Mill Hotel

The overall concept of re-contextualization for the transformation of the historic "Old Mill" building into a 4-star hotel fuses local heritage and contemporary interior design into a single whole.

The concept embraces the existing historical structure and enhances it with new materials, colors and shapes, bringing out its original qualities: Wrought iron columns rescued from the Old Mill decorate the arrival plaza, and the lobby was built from reclaimed materials from the historical building. The backdrop behind the reception is made of old machinery from the mill. Additional new materials still refer to the former industrial site but have been transferred into a new, modern architectural language that contrasts with and highlights the old. The raw atmosphere of the public areas of the Old Mill gradually transition into a softer, more private environment in the guest rooms, metal and stone giving way to wood and textiles, creating a comfortable, cosy atmosphere.

›› See page 276

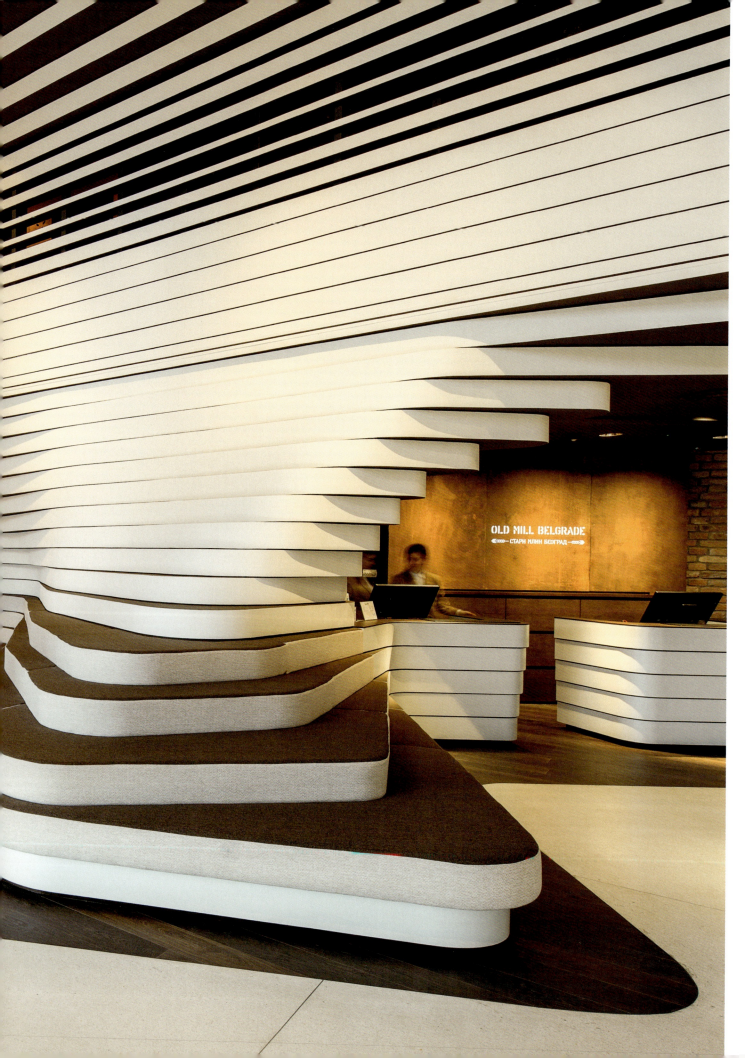

PROJECT | Hotel, adaptive reuse, interior design

OLD MILL HOTEL
BELGRADE | SERBIA

In the white city of Old Belgrade, near the banks of the River Sava, GRAFT transformed the historic building of the "Old Mill" into a 4-star hotel. The ambitious interior concept embraces the existing historical structure and enhances it with new materials, colors and shapes, bringing out its original qualities and creating a unique visual experience.

The main entrance to the hotel, with the lobby and reception, bar and restaurant, are located in the existing building complex. The new high-rise additions house the hotel rooms and suites, as well as the spa, fitness and service areas.

Visitors arrive via a new, slightly raised plaza with old granite paving and wrought iron columns rescued from the Old Mill. A new water feature neutralizes traffic noise. The lobby has an airy, authentic industrial atmosphere, and reclaimed, cleaned and repaired materials have been used from the historical building. The backdrop behind the reception is made of old machinery from the mill. Natural materials, such as oak and copper, that refer to the history of the site are used but have been transferred into a new, modern architectural language. Structurally necessary concrete incisions were kept rough to complement the overall industrial feel.

....

Left | Entrance area and reception desk with a backdrop counter made from old machines

Previous page | Reception and lobby located in the existing building complex
Right | Reception area

....

These different materials and functions are set against a giant white structure that defines the overall space and acts as a foil, bringing out the age and qualities of the different materials.

The public, raw atmosphere of the public areas of the Old Mill gradually transition into a more private and soft environment in the guest rooms. Metal and stone are replaced by wood and textiles, creating a comfortable, cosy atmosphere. The concrete structure is left exposed as a reminder of the building's industrial heritage, but layered with a wall painting that subtly alludes to the building's history and interior, inviting visitors to engage with the location. The rooms feature large low windows, customized seating, and have open, bright bathrooms. In total, there are 236 guest rooms and 14 suites with balconies on the top floors. The Old Mill building also contains a conference center with four meeting rooms, a large banquet hall and an exclusive business lounge on the top of the landmark building.

The overall concept of re-contextualization fuses local heritage and contemporary interior design into a single whole, grafting old and new, allowing the spirit of the Old Mill to live on in modern attire and creating a new local landmark in the city.

1. Reception
2. Lobby
3. Bar
4. Restaurant
5. Prefunction
6. Ballroom
7. Elevator Lobby
8. Restroom
9. Elevator Lobby

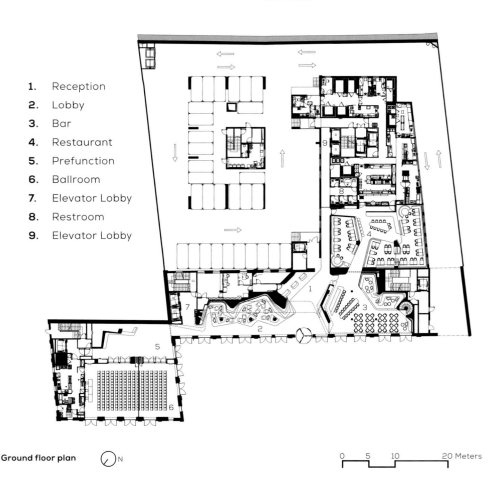

Ground floor plan N   0 5 10 20 Meters

Top | Restaurant
Left bottom | Restroom
Right bottom | Ballroom

Left top | Guest room
Left bottom | Bathroom
Right | Unclad concrete wall with 3D wall painting

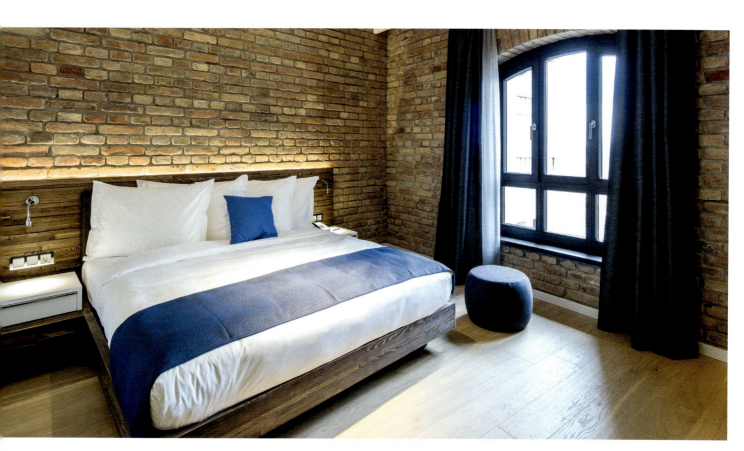

CLIENT | Soravia Group
YEAR | 2014
SIZE | 20,000m²
STATUS | Built

PROJECT | Masterplan, hotel, interior design, single-family houses

HOTEL GAMMARTH
TUNIS | TUNISIA

GRAFT was commissioned to plan a 5-star hotel and adjacent residential area in Gammarth, Tunisia, that will be a new destination for international travellers as well as locals.

On passing the gates and entering the hotel through a lush tunnel of local plants and fragrances, guests arrive beneath a spectacular concrete structure that serves as a hybrid lobby area. The arrival area blurs the boundaries between inside and outside with both indoor and outdoor check-in lounges as well as retail and service spaces. From a dune-like structure, hotel guests have a first glimpse of the ocean. The architecture is derived from the most important characteristics of the site, capturing and enhancing its specific qualities. The interaction of the sand, sea and wind is translated into a unique construction that interprets and expresses natural principles through its architecture.

Guest rooms, restaurants, pool bars and functional spaces are embedded in this dunescape, set within a garden of local plants and trees. Each dune has a cool, shaded corridor made of earth walls that guides hotel guests to their rooms. Dune-inspired patterns capture the light of the North African sun.

Each guest room has its own pool and outdoor shower as well as a rooftop terrace overlooking the hotel.

....

Right | Corridor with clay walls and shading elements

This spread | Bird's eye view of hotel and residential masterplan

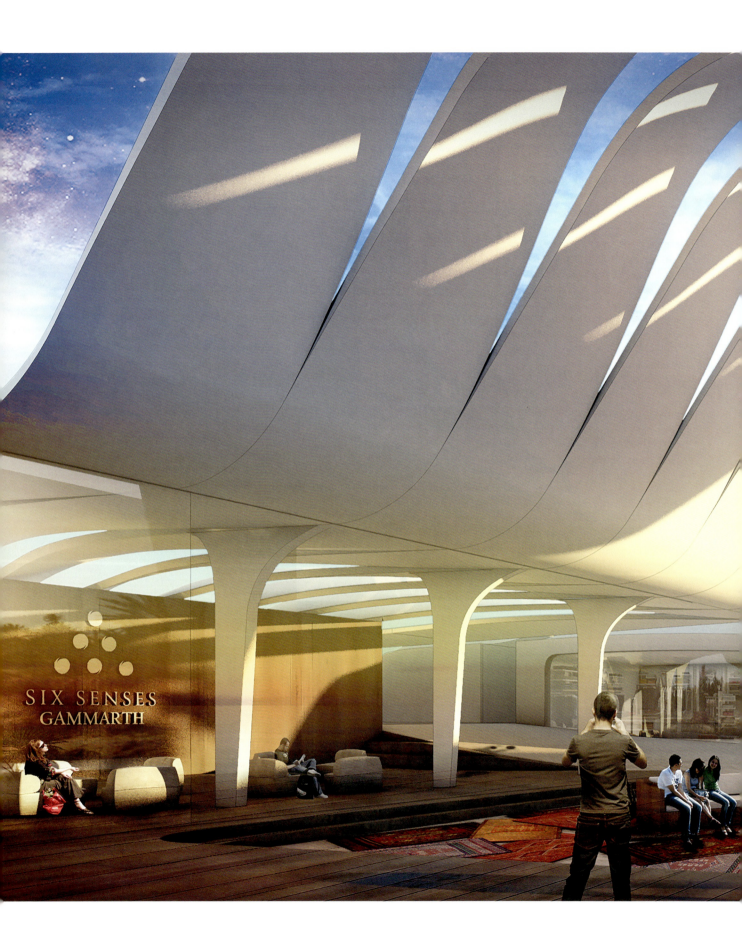

This spread | Hybrid lobby and dunescape

Left top | "Floating Villa" exterior
Left bottom | "Floating Villa" interior

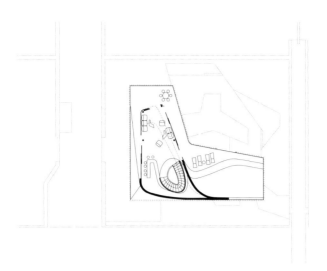

Rooftop floor plan "Floating Villa" 0 1 2 5 Meters

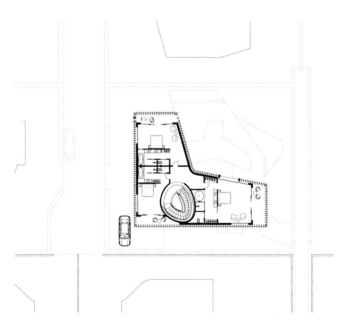

Upper floor plan "Floating Villa" 0 1 2 5 Meters

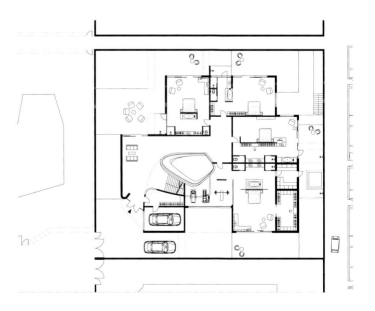

Ground floor plan "Floating Villa" 0 1 2 5 Meters

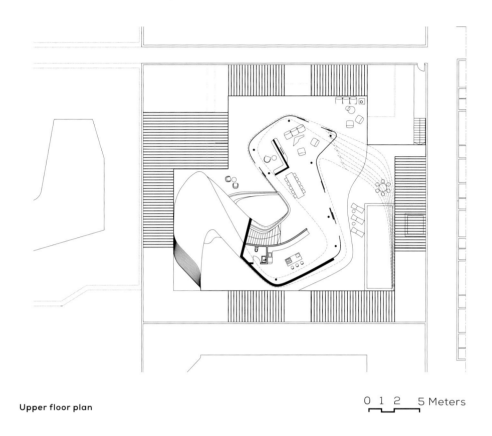

Upper floor plan

0 1 2 5 Meters

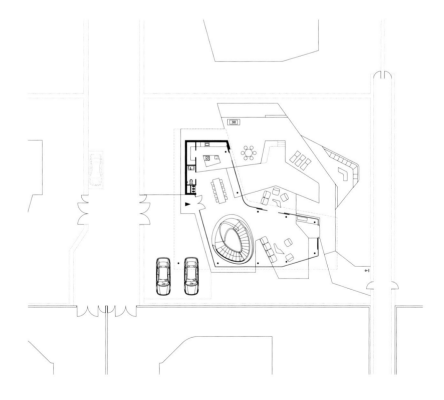

Ground floor plan

0 1 2 5 Meters

Bottom | "Plinth villa" rooftop

....

On each side of the hotel are large residential areas with two types of villa designs that provide comfortable private areas along with spacious, flexible common spaces. These spaces create opportunities for synergy effects, linking the hotel with the local community and the world outside.

Wherever possible the building makes use of local and recycled materials and transforms them into custom-made sculptures. Likewise, the restaurants use local produce from nearby farms and plantations.

A grey water recycling system makes more efficient and sustainable use of water and the heating concept is designed to be climate-adaptive, with predominantly north-facing windows to avoid solar heat gain, cooling ceilings for basic air conditioning and earth-covered concrete roof slabs to ensure sufficient thermal mass and buffer heat transfer to improve the indoor room climate.

———

Right top | Rooftop bar, dunescape at night
Left bottom | Spa
Right bottom | Restaurant at night

CLIENT | Confidential
YEAR | 2013
SIZE | 5,000,000m²
STATUS | In progress

PROJECT | Family house, hotel

FAMILY HOUSE SANKT AUGUSTIN
SANKT AUGUSTIN | GERMANY

The Family House is a charity that provides space and a home for families whose hospitalized children are in the process of receiving medical treatment.

The house, a dynamic bending structure, finds its resting position on top of a small hill in the surrounding topography.

On the ground floor, a long table in the center of the public area serves as a joint space for the entire house. It is here that parents have the opportunity to engage in conversation with each other while preparing meals together, creating a reciprocal sense of support and understanding.
An elongated interactive ramp in the central area connects the interior communal spaces to a large outdoor terrace and serves multiple communal uses. It can be a landscape with spaces for sitting and lying down, a playground for children, a performance stage, as well as a quiet area for parents to work.

Each room enjoys spectacular views over the fields of Sankt Augustin, and all 25 apartments face the setting sun. Custom-made furniture is integrated into the window frame of every room.

The entire structure is more of an iconographic building sculpture than a conventional guest house, and the lightness of the gesture serves as an expression of hope and confidence in difficult times.

Left | Street view

Left top | Back view
Right top | Side view

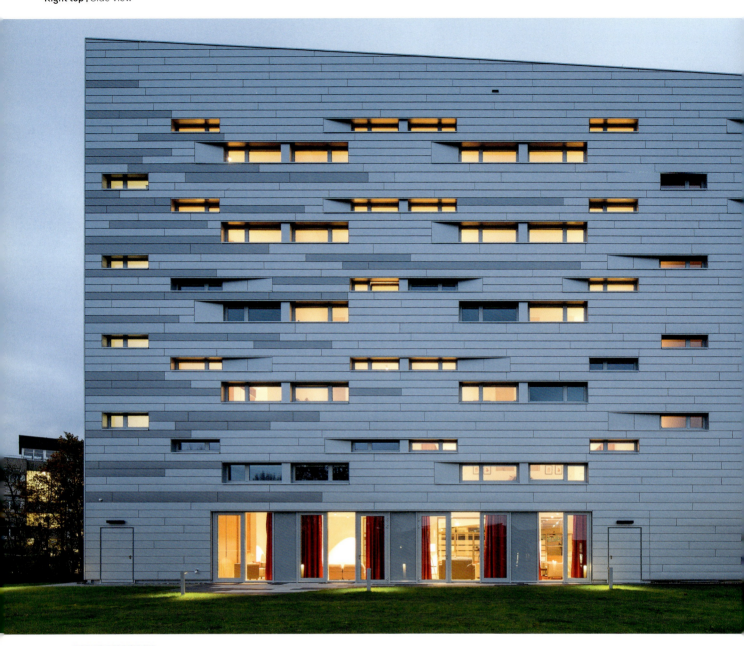

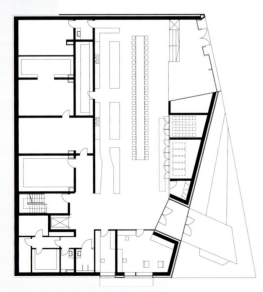

Ground floor plan

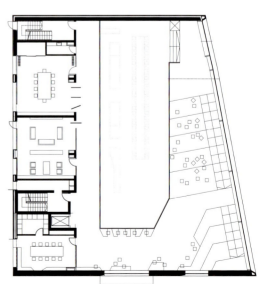

1st floor plan

CLIENT | McDonald's Kinderhilfe
YEAR | 2014
SIZE | 1,900m²
STATUS | Built

This spread | Community spaces

PROJECT | Hotel and landscape design

HOTEL AND SPA SEEZEITLODGE
BOSTALSEE | GERMANY

The Hotel and Spa Seezeitlodge occupies an advantageous position in its natural surroundings, overlooking the serene lake Bostalsee from a wooded promontory. GRAFT's design aims to build on and enrich the character of the location.

The building figure is a product of the surrounding topography. The hotel connects the realm of the wood with the expanse of the lake, mediating between the land and the water.

Guests arrive at the hotel through oak woodland, barely seeing the lake. The path to the hotel leads on towards two green hills on which the main section of the two-story hotel rests. The lobby is situated beneath it at the natural gap between the hills, revealing a breathtaking view over the lake as one enters. The lobby frames the sunset which in turn animates the space with the cycle of nature. An open-air terrace with fireplace offers guests an opportunity to enjoy the evening spectacle.

From the lobby, guests can proceed onto the restaurant, bar and reading room or to the conference spaces and spa. These functional spaces, as well as the administrative facilities, are embedded in the topography of the hilly landscape. The 2,000m²-large spa and wellness area faces onto the surrounding woodland to create a sheltered, private environment of high-quality indoor and outdoor spaces. The restaurant, conference areas and some

....

parts of the spa open onto the lake, and enjoy an incredible panoramic view. The 100 guest rooms and suites are located on the two upper floors: the rooms on the southwest enjoy the setting sun in the evening, while those on the northwest side see the rising sun in the morning. The suites at the north end of the hotel building offer spectacular views over the cape and the lake.

The below-ground infrastructure linking the administrative areas, spa and conference areas is minimal. A penthouse and bar will be constructed on the roof at a later stage. The woodland on the west side has been thinned out to provide more views of the lake and the wood used for the façade of the hotel. The timber slats of the façade have been charred, lending the building a silvery-black shine. The gross building area totals approximately 11,800m², including the outdoor wellness areas and the covered parking spaces. GRAFT's design is a response to the spirit of the place, and builds on its qualities to create a new harmonious whole. The result is a travel destination with a special identity of its own.

CLIENT | HOTELKULTUR GmbH & Co. KG
SIZE | 12,000m²
YEAR | 2016
STATUS | Under construction

PROJECT | Mobile brewery, beer garden, event space, temporary architecture

BRLO BRWHOUSE
BERLIN | GERMANY

In Berlin, on the site of "Urbane Mitte" between the eastern and western parts of Gleisdreieck Park, GRAFT designed and planned a mobile brewery and beer garden. The building for BRLO BRWHOUSE combines a restaurant and bar, beer garden and events space with a craft brewery and administration spaces, and is remarkable for its modular container architecture.

GRAFT designed a freestanding building made of shipping containers, similar to the two "Platoon Kunsthalle" container constructions opened in Seoul in 2009 and in Berlin in 2012. The pre-fabricated containers are altered individually according to their function and are stacked to form a mobile home base for the young local brewing company BRLO. The building is designed for temporary usage over a period of 3-5 years, and if necessary can easily be dismantled and reconstructed at another location.

Four containers long and three containers high, the block provides about 600m² of floor space, sufficient for the brewery equipment, as well as room for guests, events, and administration. To the west, a vertically placed container contains a staircase and functions as the entrance to the office spaces. A second, inclined container at the end of the west side provides outside access to a gallery level. The utilitarian character of the container architecture is emphasized by its anthracite color.

Left | Beer garden at night

This spread | Opening event of beer garden

This spread | Mobile brewery and event space

CLIENT | Braukunst Berlin GmbH
SIZE | 600m²
YEAR | 2016
STATUS | Under construction

PROJECT | Youth hostel, refurbishment, new construction

YOUTH HOSTEL MUNICH CITY
MUNICH | GERMANY

The Bavarian association of German youth hostels invited five architecture offices to design the modernization of one of Germany's oldest hostels located in the center of Munich. Primary focus was given to the extension of the existing building with an innovative and high quality design that embodies the fundamental values of the association in a new way.

GRAFT's winning concept highlights the idea of "Experiencing Community" in which modern architecture plays a central role in enabling exchange and communication while simultaneously remaining true to the principles of travelling simply, youthful curiosity and the thirst for encounters. In the interior, in particular, the design pairs the local iconography of wooden buildings with innovative design. In the context of changing habits and practices, the new youth hostel builds a bridge between origins and departure.

The design proposes relocating the main entrance of the new youth hostel to face "Winthirplatz".
A new building closes off the perimeter block, its calm, regular façade respecting the characteristics of the district. In its face, however, a two-story amorphous lobby has been carved, creating a dramatic entrance space that simultaneously announces the building to its surroundings.

....

Right | Lobby and community spaces wirth digital walls

This spread | Street perspective

This spread | Guest room

....

Natural elements of the square and the inner courtyard are translated into an amorphous, landscaped architecture that ties together the indoor and outdoor spaces. The materials relate to regional construction methods.

The complex is large enough to host numerous visitors at the same time and symbolizes the basic idea of "Experiencing Community": the design intentionally combines the functions of the lobby, dining room and seminar spaces into a joint interior space.

For today's young people, community also takes place increasingly in virtual spaces. The lobby is therefore not only a physical communal space but also a virtual "cloud" in which interactions between guests are augmented by simple devices – a graphics "black board", QR codes, mini screens and map projections, as well as Facebook and Twitter. The rooms are the second major identifying factor for this new generation youth hostel, combining modern design and flexible room arrangements with robust functionality.

The façade of the historic old building at the Wendl-Dietrich-Strasse will be renovated in accordance with conservation guidelines. The distinctive arches at the entrance will be made usable by means of glazed fronts. The entire youth hostel is designed for disabled access, making all its qualities available to everyone.

―――

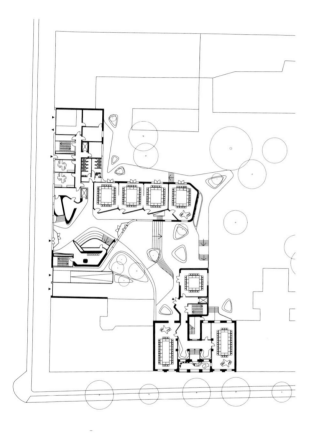

Ground floor plan

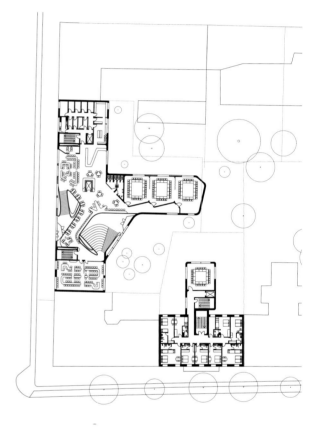

1st floor plan

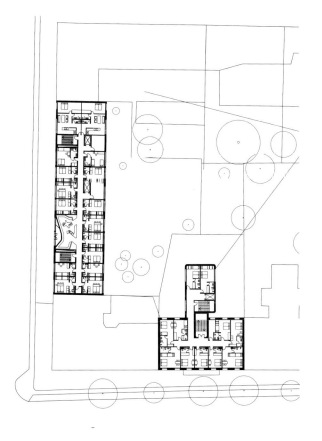
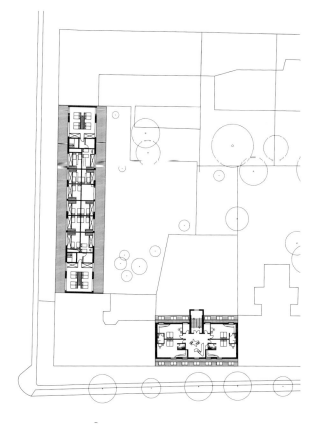

2nd floor plan

6th floor plan

0 1 5 10 Meters

CLIENT | Deutsches Jugendherbergswerk
YEAR | 2014
SIZE | 10,500m²
STATUS | Under construction

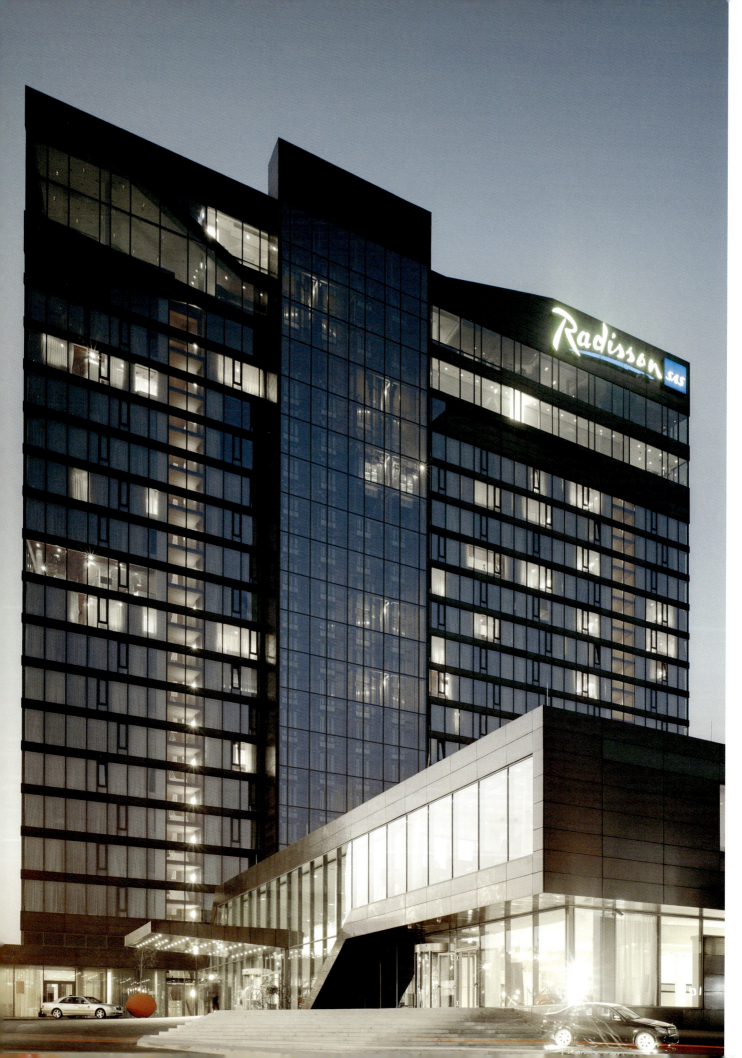

PROJECT | Hotel, casino, high-rise

HOTEL IVERIA
TBILISI | GEORGIA

―――――

The hotel and casino is a conversion of an existing 20-story high-rise building from the 1960s as a mixed-use facility with 34,170m² of gross floor area on a land parcel of 10,840m². The Hotel Iveria accommodates 249 rooms, including 44 business class rooms, 15 suites and one executive suite, as well as an Italian restaurant called Filini, the Surface Restaurant and Lounge Bar, a conference center with 10 fully-equipped meeting rooms and a sub-dividable ballroom with a maximum capacity of 450 persons. A bank office and travel agency complete the program of spaces.

The project's goal is to transform an urban landmark building of the so-called international style by anchoring it in the local environment of the city center and reconnecting it to the world of today. In many former communist countries, architectural icons from "socialist" times are being transformed and countries are seeking to express their own identity with a renewed sense of confidence. The project is a bold, optimistic statement

....

Left | Entrance to Iveria hotel and casino

....

demonstrating Georgia's and Tbilisi's position as a modern city while respecting the history of Georgia, including its more recent past – a project that embodies the principles of GRAFT.

The design respects the basic form and placement of the typical modernist high-rise while introducing strong interventions that heighten its qualities: the ground and first floors have been gutted and given a new base that relates the lobby and restaurant to its surroundings, while the top two storys have been transformed into spa and wellness facilities with a spectacular view over the city and to the Caucasus Mountains beyond. The exterior has been re-clad with a sleek skin of rhythmic curtain-wall glazing, while the interiors refer to local traditions such as the wooden balconies of Tbilisi (hotel rooms), the local sulphur bathing culture (spa) or the wood relief-work, carpeting and niches in the restaurants and bars. Transformed, abstracted images of grapes are used as a decorative device throughout the project.

Georgia as a country at the intersection of cultures and trade routes is rediscovering its role as an international hub and a place for exchange between the East and West. The prominent project was an opportunity to help reclaim past traditions and participate in their transformation and definition, linking the global with the local in a two-way process.

———

Right | Hôtel lobby

This spread | Casino

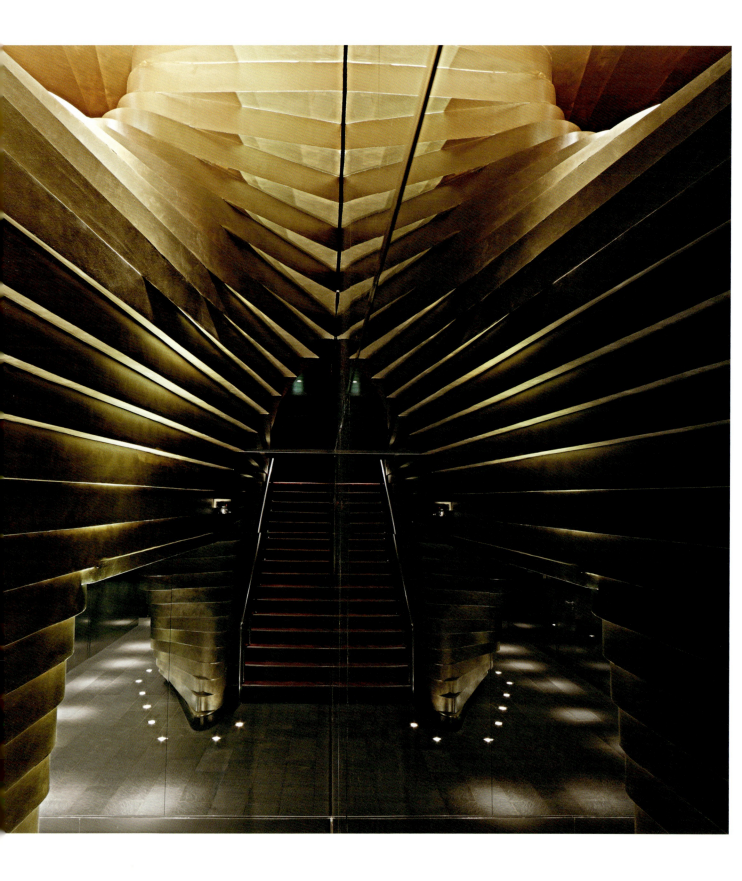

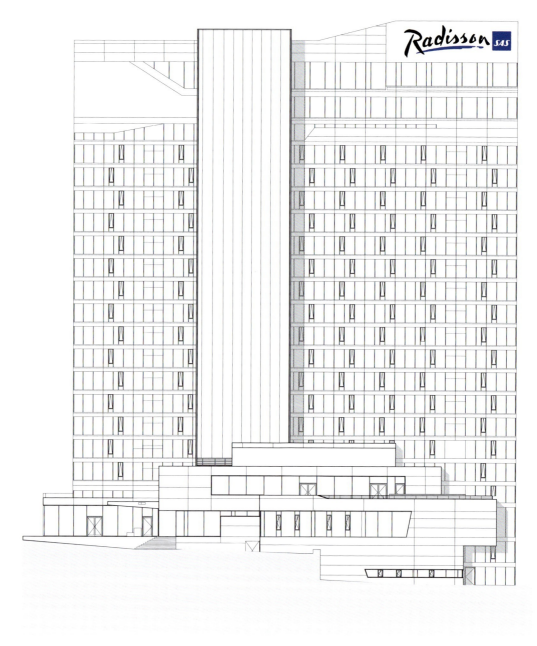

Hotel elevation

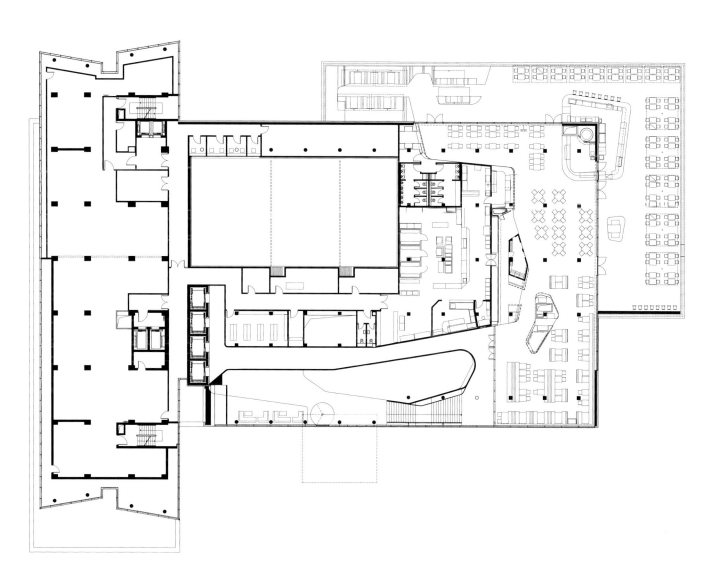

Ground floor plan N

Left | Guest room

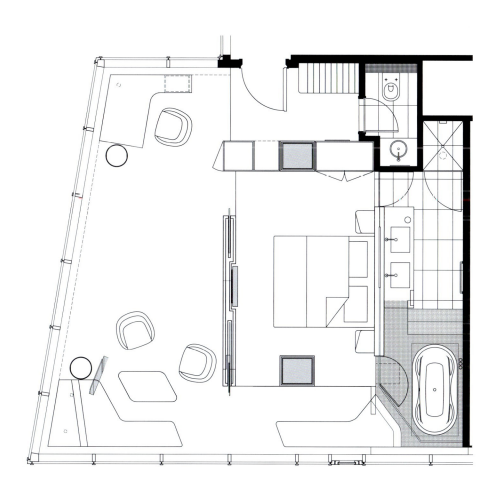

Guest room floor plan

Top | Swimming pool and spa area
Left and right botttom | Skybar with spa area and swimming pool in the background

CLIENT | Development Solutions
YEAR | 2008
SIZE | 34,200m²
STATUS | Built

This spread | Rose Square

CLIENT | New Office LLC
YEAR | 2016
SIZE | 8,000m²
STATUS | In progress

In 2016 GRAFT won a competition to design Rose Square, one of the few public spaces in the city of Tbilisi. It is uniquely situated between the Radisson Blu "Hotel Iveria" and Radisson Telegraph, with an open view to the north of the city. Currently it is little more than an in-between space used for parking.

The new Rose Square is conceived as a folded surface, floating above ground. It hovers over the city center, connecting the different levels and areas. The new square is partly inclined, connecting it with the underground areas the square was originally built on in the 1970s and creating a new retail and restaurant area, along with sunken gardens. An underground pedestrian route links the hotel to the Boulevard Rustaveli. The design picks up the distinct features of the capital's terraced topography and revives the potential of a varied urban landscape.

The two-level public space creates a space of calm while guiding the flow of visitors through a continuous landscape. Cut-outs in the square's surface connect urban routes passing through the space and additional design elements demarcate places to stop and stay at the east and west ends of the square. The new Rose Square is a multifunctional public space, offering different features and facilities for visitors. The main area at the very heart of the area is conceived as an urban amphitheater, a forum for the public as well as for spontaneous performances.

The area in front of the Radisson Blu Hotel in Tbilisi, Georgia, is the Cour d'Honneur of the Hotel Iveria with a vibrant character and seasonal water elements. In the warm Georgian summers, the water mirrors the sky and fountains refresh passing visitors, while in winter the space can be used for ice skating.

PROJECT | Interior design hotel and multi-family condominium

W HOTEL
NEW YORK | USA

The W Hotel & Residences is the largest global-brand luxury hotel and residences project in downtown New York and the first W residential development in Manhattan. Located at 123 Washington Street, one block from the site of the new Freedom Tower, the W Downtown is a 58-story building with 255 hotel rooms, 233 condominium units, a restaurant, bars, lounges and open-air roof garden. The interior design is best described as classical modernism with a twist – on the one hand understatement and clarity, on the other new, fresh and even futuristic ideas on comfort and luxury. We call it Punk Minimalism. The project offers a glimpse of the future of living, working and visiting in one of the most vibrant locations in the world.

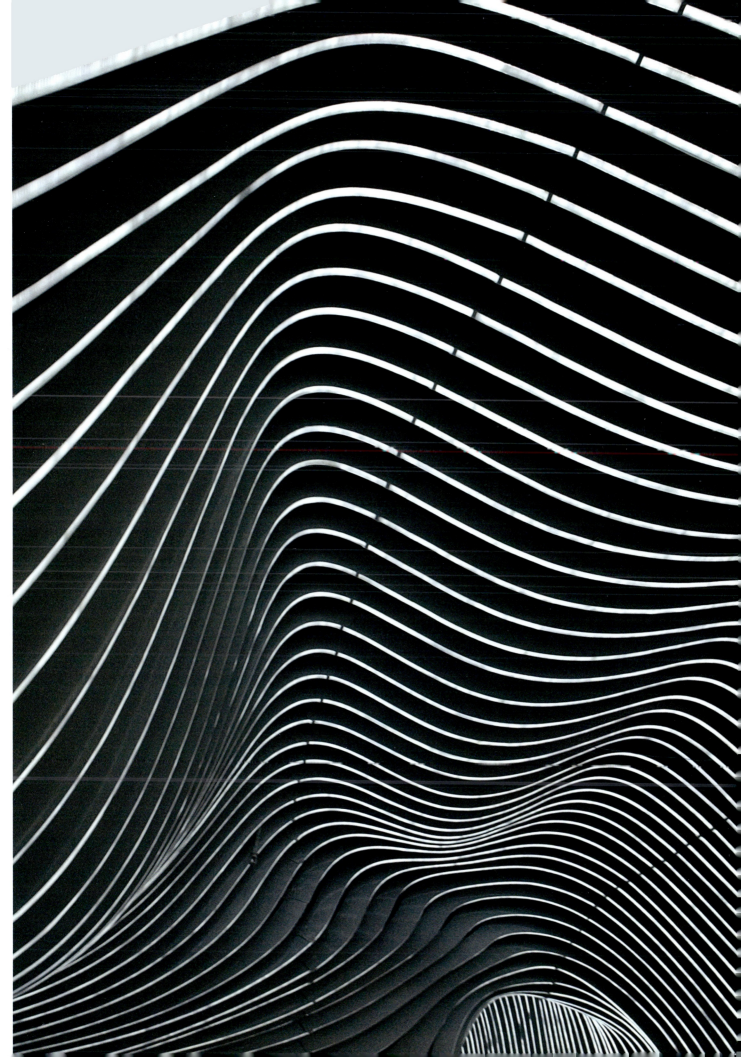

This spread | Lobby and bar area

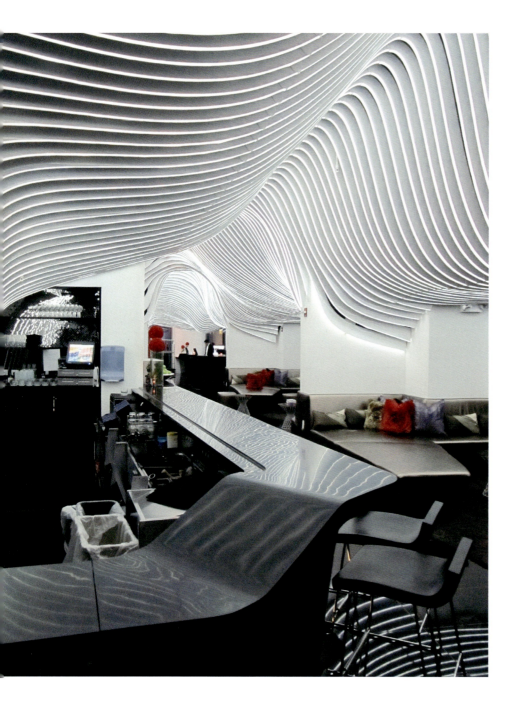

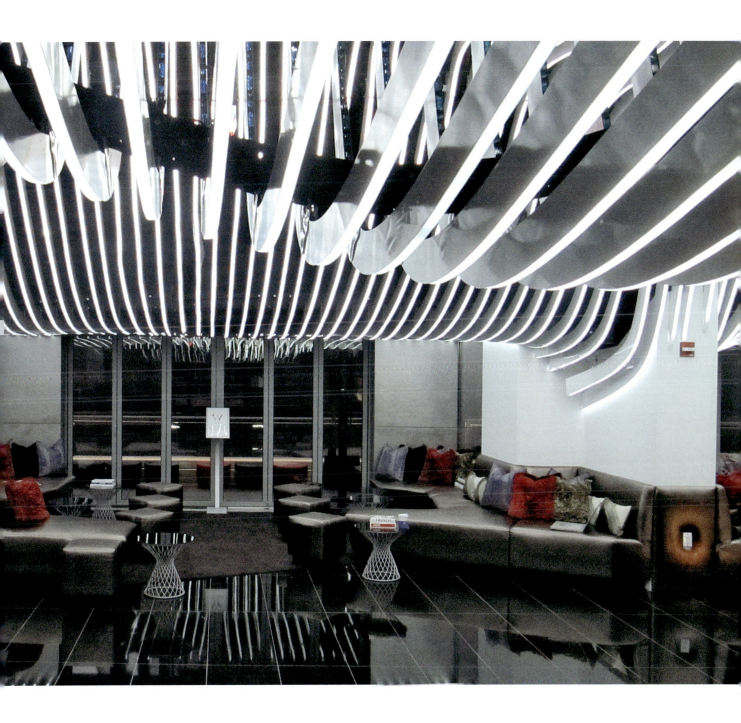

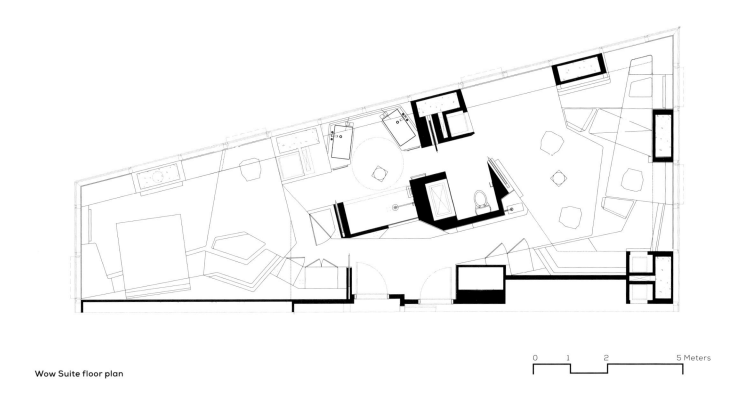

Wow Suite floor plan

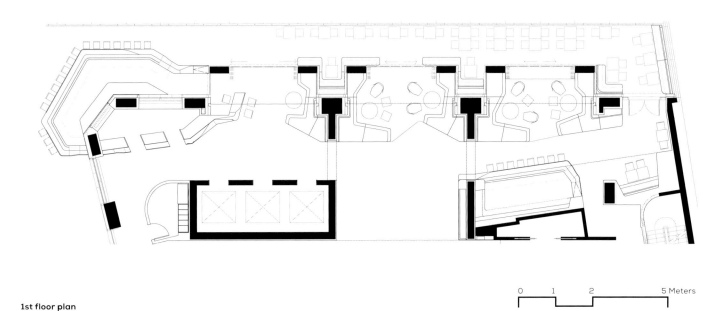

1st floor plan

CLIENT | The Monian Group
YEAR | 2009
SIZE | 34,000m²
STATUS | Built

PROJECT | Hotel, high-rise, urban planning, mixed use

VERTICAL VILLAGE
DUBAI | U.A.E.

Vertical Village is a residential, hotel and entertainment development that harnesses the most powerful renewable energy source in the desert: the sun. Arranged to reduce solar gain and maximize solar production, the buildings are massed as self-shading slabs at the north end of the site on the east-west axis to reduce low-angle sun penetration. At the southern end of the site, a vast array of solar collectors is optimally angled toward the sun, facing the main public strip as a potent gesture of the development's sustainable aspirations, which are confirmed by its LEED Gold rated performance. The solar roof behaves much like a leaf, with veins that divide the solar field into serviceable units and also transport energy, in this case hot water, back to the building where the energy is used to significantly reduce the need for air conditioning and to provide hot water. Beneath the roof lies an urban-scale entertainment district of cinemas, restaurants, shops and a theater. The scale and degree of privacy transitions from the main entertainment strip to the south and the residential and hotel towers to the north.

Left | View from West
Right | View from South

The sculptural, inclined, sliced wedges of the residential and hotel buildings give each building a unique, identifiable appearance, and together form a distinctive skyline that shifts as one drives by. As one approaches the complex, the spaces between the slabs are revealed, then meld together, disappear and reappear, creating a theatrical effect, a subtle and poetic reference to the entertainment functions within the complex.

CLIENT | Confidential
YEAR | 2004
SIZE | 390,000m²
STATUS | In progress
IN COLLABORATION WITH | Brad Pitt

PROJECT | Restaurant, bar and club

CITY CENTER'S ARIA
LAS VEGAS | USA

City Center is a mixed-use, 18 million square feet development by MGM Mirage that features buildings by several world-renowned architects. The unique 76 acre urban resort is located in the heart of Las Vegas' famed Strip and is a collection of luxury hotels, condominiums, casinos, shopping facilities, and entertainment venues, which include Aria, Vdara, the Mandarin Oriental, Veer Towers and Crystals. To date, it is the largest privately financed development in the history of the United States and is also the largest LEED-certified project in the world. Located at the base of Aria, the main resort and casino, the pool deck is a lush tropical lagoon with an intimate sanctuary of cabanas around a luxurious pool area in the midst of the larger vision of the City Center. The structures fuse the stunning beauty and richness of the tropics with the simplicity of contemporary culture.

The architecture is conceived as a series of overlapping contours, creating fluid transitions and establishing a spatial hierarchy for the separate lounge areas. The pool deck can cater for 1,500 guests and consists of 52 separate cabanas, two bars, a restaurant, retail facilities and a European pool lounge.

....

Right | Pool area and Breeze Café Restaurant

....

The various buildings, designed as a family of structures set within a landscape, permit individual variation while unifying the overall composition of the pool deck and resort through the use of a similar palette of materials and formal relationships between them. Materials such as Massaranduba wood and various textiles were chosen both for their visual and haptic qualities as well as for environmental and ecological reasons. The interplay between monolithic forms and panelized sections creates unique figure-group relationships.

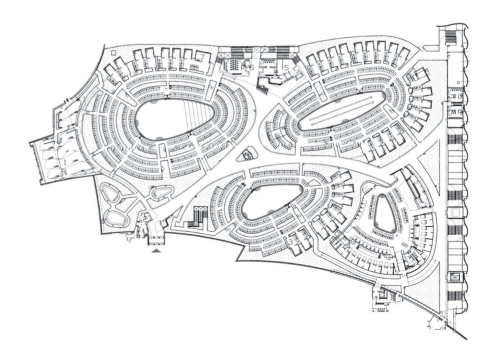

1. Breeze Café
2. Pool retail
3. Cabanas
4. Pool lounge
5. Pool bar
6. Pool bar restaurant
7. Double cabanas

Site plan N

0 5 10 20 Meters

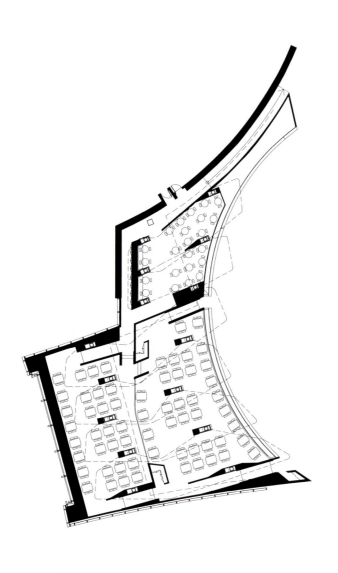

Breeze Café N   0 1 2 5 Meters

BREEZE CAFÉ

The Breeze Café and pool bar is located at the eastern end of the lagoon. The structure is inspired by the cooling experience of Mangrove forests. Large canopies provide shade, while simultaneously allowing free air flow through the openings between the roof structures, creating an enticing play of light and shadows in the space. The interplay of warm, comforting wood and sculptural white plaster surfaces enhances the experience of an opulent refuge from the sizzling sun.

POOL BAR

The pool bar in the center of the area is modeled on the idea of a dwelling sheltered beneath a cliff. The large projecting overhang of the bar provides cool shelter from the sun. The monolithic white structure is open, its roof extending an inviting gesture to guests and revealing a welcoming wood interior with an abstract image of a canyon behind the bar.

LIQUID POOL LOUNGE

The third architectural element is a secluded cove at the western end of the pool area: an adult-only escape to another world of relaxation. This refuge continues the material palette of the other zones but uses a different architectural and spatial language, setting it apart from the adjacent areas. The Liquid Pool Lounge is operated by the Light Group and the rear of the bar features original artwork by the artist Camron Slocum from Los Angeles.

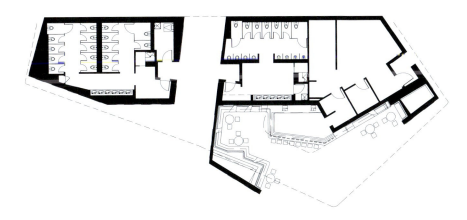

Liquid Pool Lounge

CLIENT | MGM Mirage
YEAR | 2009
SIZE | 17,000m²
STATUS | Built

PROJECT | Interior design

HOTEL Q!
BERLIN | GERMANY

Hotels are home away from home. For a short while they offer visitors another world in which they can inhabit new identities, re-tell their own individual story and catch a glimpse of the future. Hotels have the ability to seduce, to overturn old habits and inspire new rituals.

Over the past decade a new kind of hotel has emerged that offers a different experience to that of standardized hotel chains or utilitarian tourist accommodation. These "design hotels" aim to be unique, authentic and of their place, offering the modern cosmopolitan traveller a memorable experience.

Around the corner from the buzzing Kurfürstendamm strip on Knesebeckstrasse, GRAFT designed a hotel landscape that challenges the classical spatial canon, proposing in its place a folding topographical structure. Following a tectonic logic, a horizontal landscape of folded and distorted objects creates hybrid zones with dual functional purposes. An inclined section serves both as a separating wall and a piece of furniture. The section that rises out of the floor is both a surface

....

Left | Lobby sitting niche

This spread | Exterior view of reception and bar

Right | Hotel bar
Bottom | Sketches

for circulation as well as part of a space emerging from underneath the building. Rather than dividing the space into multiple distinct spaces, the flow of this internal landscape creates an open interconnected interior. The topographical treatment of the design maximizes the versatility of the program and creates a continuous flow of form and space. The spatial narrative departs from conventional perceptual experiences and allows for ambiguous readings of the space.

To achieve the distinctive forms of the design and fulfill the necessary functional requirements, the architects searched intensively for an appropriate material before settling on Marmoleum Real 3127, a product by the Forbo Flooring GmbH.

GRAFT's design invites the inhabitants to become a participant in this landscape, to adapt how they interact with architecture and furniture by "walking up the walls" in order to take a seat above the distinguished crowd. Beds seamlessly blend into bathtubs, offering themselves like hot springs bubbling up from the ground, so that visitors can slow down and dream – with their eyes wide open.

The Hotel opened in April 2004 and encompasses a lobby, lounge and spa, 72 rooms, 4 studios and 1 penthouse.

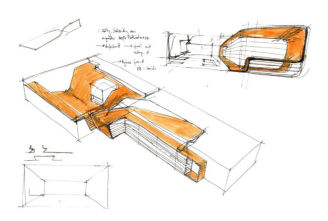
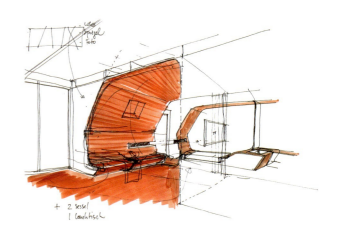

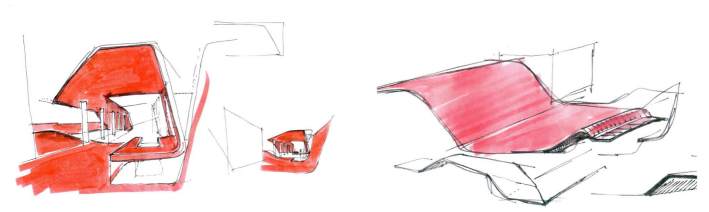

Left top | Spa
Left bottom | Restroom detail
Right | Spa

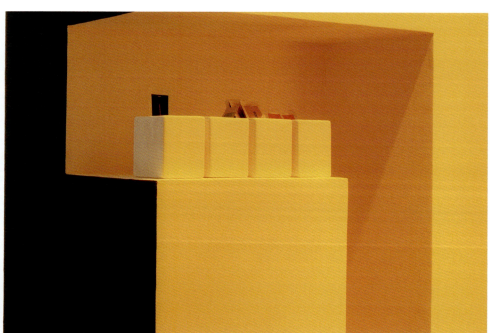

Left | Bedroom
Right | Bedroom with integrated bathtub

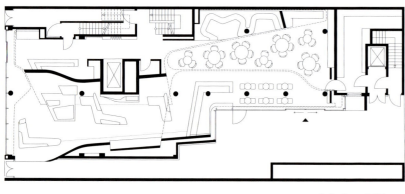

Ground floor plan

2nd and 3rd floor plan

CLIENT | Wanzl GmbH & Co. KG
YEAR | 2004
SIZE | 3,200m²
STATUS | Built

PROJECT | First prize competition, hotel, residential development

HOTEL LOFER
LOFER | AUSTRIA

The Hotel Lofer is the first "premium common good resort" of its kind and encompasses a hotel complex, café, villa, staff hotel and premium residence area, as well as a community-oriented enterprise.

The design of the complex in Lofer near Salzburg (Austria) was awarded first prize in an open competition in which the local population were invited to participate in the judging.

Building in the Alps entails respecting the characteristic cultural landscape and deep-rooted sense of identity while introducing new impulses for its future. New architecture must achieve a balance between change and nostalgia, between innovation and being of its place. GRAFT's design preserves the historical façades while integrating cutting-edge architecture. The innovative new additions draw on the larch cladding of local vernacular timber buildings and apply it to a prismatic, sculptural form. Each of the buildings responds in different ways to the genius loci, the roof forms adjusting to fit into the surrounding context of the village.

....

Left | Lobby
Right | Guest room

Environmental sustainability was a central concern of the design: together with the international engineering firm BuroHappold, a complex was designed that meets the needs of a modern hotel without polluting soil, air or water. Energy and water consumption is minimized through a "lean-mean-green" strategy using a combination of modern, energy-efficient technology and renewable energy sources.
In addition to harnessing natural resources such as rain, snow and sun, the façade and building meet stringent sustainability criteria.

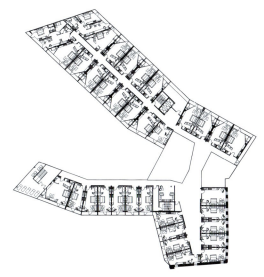

2nd floor plan

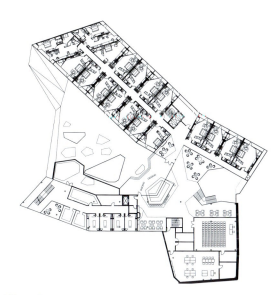

1st floor plan

Ground floor plan N

0 5 10   20 Meters

This spread | Spa area

CLIENT | Private client
SIZE | 16,800m²
YEAR | 2014
STATUS | In progress

PROJECT | Hotel, interior design

THE EMPEROR
BEIJING | CHINA

Right in the historical center of Beijing the Emperor is located along the first tree lined alley on the Eastern side of the Forbidden City, adjacent to the majestic "Ning He" Temple from the Qing Dynasty,

The existing building interior was stripped to the bare concrete prior to the creation of the hotel. From this clean slate were crafted 60 rooms, a restaurant and lounge, and a spectacular roof terrace, all encompassing an area of 4800m².

The conceptual genesis of the redesign was the consideration of the volume of the existing building as a "white mass" into which the rooms and hallways were carved. After the first "rough cut" which addressed the main spaces, a second trace of carvings, a striation of colorful suede was introduced. This striation is combining a multiplicity of architectural elements as one moves through the entire building, joining the elements within with one architectural language.

In the lobby the striation begins as an extended sofa protruding into the entryway where guests can lounge and welcome new arrivals.
From here it swings up the walls to create displays for local news and city info and then bends into the hallways where Beijing's history and Chinese culture is described on flat screens and in sound caves.

....

Left | Wall element with integrated sitting niche

This spread | Guest room

Top | Exterior view
Bottom | Guest room

....

These sound caves are deeply carved out areas of the hotel hallways; where, clad in lush suede, they invite guests to pause and listen to traditional Chinese opera as it drifts through the hotel. Continuing on, the striation is present on the doors to the guest suites where graphic abstractions of portraits of emperors replace room numbers. In this way the guest room keys facilitate a journey through history as each room is named after and portrays a different emperor.

Throughout the hotel the expressive colors of the suede striations change according to floors and suite types, allowing returning guests to explore and find their personal color preferences.

Inside the guest suites the striation morphs again, swings to the horizontal along the walls to become sofas and finally the bed. Within the rooms, the suede is imprinted with the rooflines of the Forbidden City, which continues over the glass enclosure of the bathrooms. A seductive narrative of concealment and revelation plays out on the partially frosted glass at once flooding the bathrooms with daylight while providing a minimum of privacy between the bedroom and the shower.
The Emporor provides multifaceted food and entertainment facilities.
On the lower level, the "SHI" (Chinese for EAT) Restaurant is accessible from the hotel by the central staircase. "SHI" is divided into three areas: the western area encompasses a variety of booth seating, as well as a banquet table with a capacity of 24 seats. In the center area, a central bar and food counter serves as pivot point. The Eastern part serves as lounge; here daybeds separated by translucent curtains are arranged around a central sofa feature with integrated fireplace.

The curtains play with the theme of concealment and revelation present throughout the entire hotel. They are translucent and on each is painted a single stroke of the Chinese character for EAT. When viewed from a perpendicular angle the single strokes align and the full character becomes legible.

On the opposite end of the hotel, the roof terrace is another highlight of the hotel. From the hotel bar "HE" (Chinese for DRINK) guests enjoy an unparalleled view of the Beijing skyline with the golden roofs of the Forbidden City looming in the foreground. Hotel guests can enjoy the reserved spa called "Yue" (Chinese for "Pleasant") and "Jing" (Chinese for "Spirit"), the gym on the eastern part of the roof level. Aside massage rooms and a shallow pool, it features an elevated rooftop hot tub, where guests can soak in panoramic views of Beijing.

———

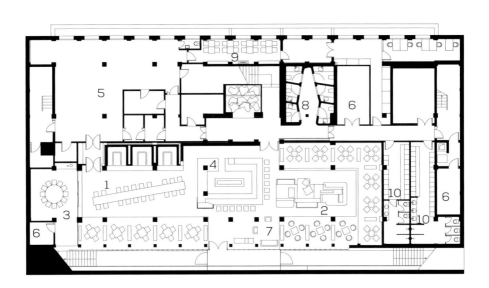

Ground floor plan

1. Dining room
2. Lounge
3. VIP room
4. Bar
5. Kitchen
6. Storage
7. Reception
8. Lavatory
9. Kitchen
10. Locker room

0 1 2 5 Meters

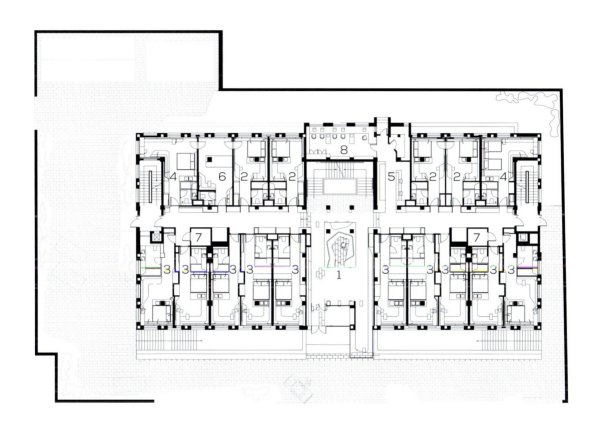

1st floor plan

1. Reception
2. Normal room
3. Deluxe room
4. Junior suite
5. Reception
6. Extension
7. Storage
8. Security room

Left | Lounge Bar
Right | Daybed with integrated tables

Left | The rooftop terrace with bar, spa and gym

CLIENT | Beijing Dacheng Yongan Zhiya Co., Ltd
YEAR | 2008
SIZE | 4,800m²
STATUS | Built

PROJECT | Hotel design

SAMANA LUXURY RESORT
SAMANA | DOMINICAN REPUBLIC

In the remote and northern most part of the Dominican Republic lays the peninsula of Samana. Secluded with untouched archaic beauty, the piece of earth has not changed since Columbus discovered this paradise on his second journey.

GRAFT was asked to design a luxurious resort and spa complex in a very lush and steeply sloped valley here that opens singularly to the ocean. The decision was made to keep the valley floor with its Palmeraie untouched and pure and to develop the architecture nestled and grafted into the northern hillside, looking out onto an unspoiled landscape and ocean. A rhizome of hotel suites, connected through funiculars with a reception area at the bottom, stretch out over the valley slope. Equipped with private pools, each suite has a spectacular view over the valley and the ocean with its dramatically hued sunsets.

The spa is located on the other side of the valley. Cut into the hillside in a long horizontal groove, it features a generous enfilade of spaces with thrilling panoramic scenarios towards the ocean and beach.

Right | Hotel suites grafted into northern hillside

This spread | Samana spa

CLIENT | Nader Group
YEAR | 2006
SIZE | 14,450m²
STATUS | In progress
IN COLLABORATION WITH | Brad Pitt

PROJECT | Restaurant design

STACK RESTAURANT & BAR
LAS VEGAS | USA

An enticing canyoning landscape is generated through undulating striations of seating, layered wall and bar, utilizing the generous 19" height capacity to produce a telescopic effect in depth.

The horizontal layers are peeled from one another, creating variation in patterning, cantilevering and velocity.

This effect forms a visible invitation to the space, drawing the visitor in, and gradually frames multiple spatial readings, keeping the guest inside. The canyon wall is embedded with a lighting effect which reveals a random pixelated pattern once one has journeyed inside the restaurant and looks back out from the interior of the restaurant.

In order to create a dense and consistent atmospheric intensity, GRAFT chose quarter-figured African mahogany wood panelling for the layered canyon, giving both warmth to the space and translating the canyon feel into a contemporary formal solution.

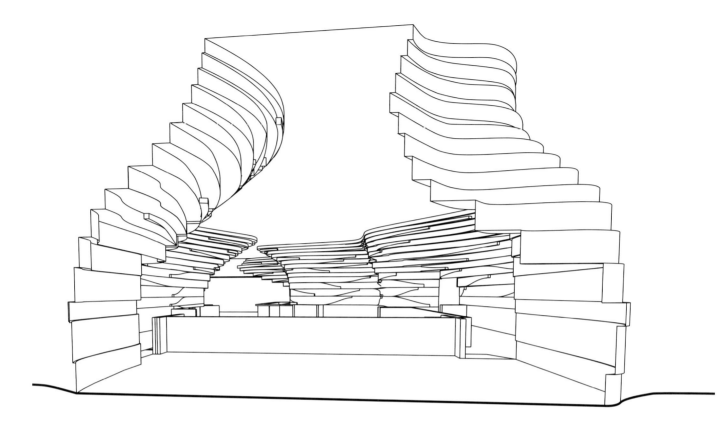

Perspective section

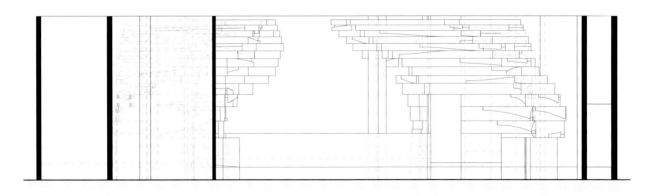

Section

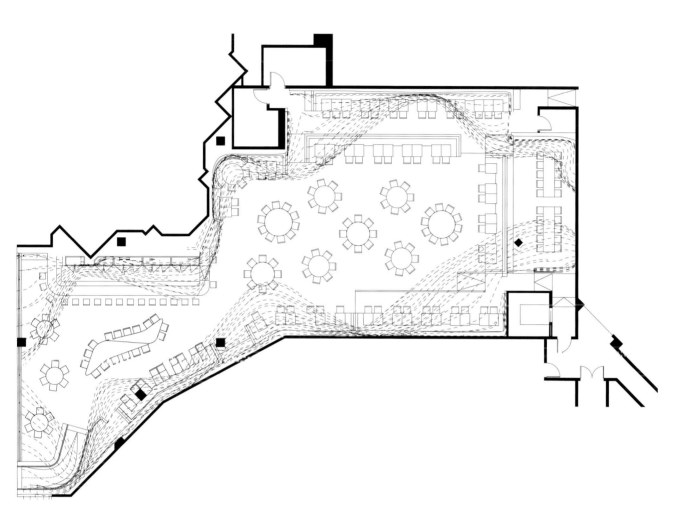

Floor plan

1. Casino
2. Elevated Dining
3. Private Dining
4. Main Dining
5. Food Service
6. Bar
7. Lounge
8. Lavatory
9. Storage
10. Entrance from Kitchen

Left | Details
Right | Restaurant

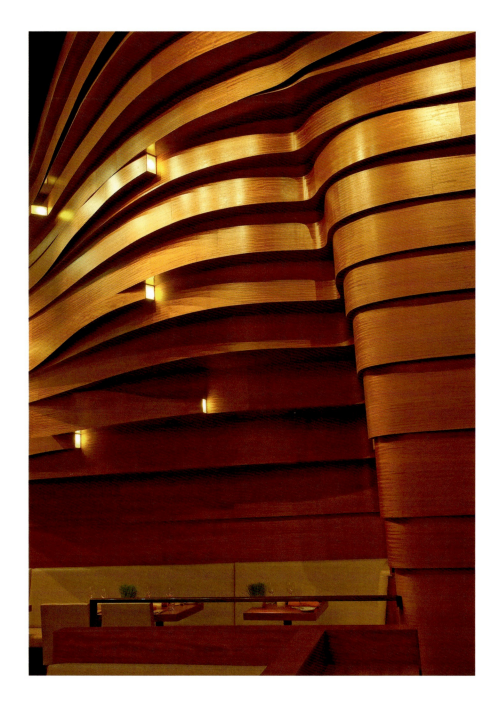

CLIENT | MGM Mirage Design Group
YEAR | 2008
SIZE | 700m²
STATUS | Built

PROJECT | Urban planning, mixed used

DESERT CANYON RESORT
DUBAI | U.A.E

Conceived as a singular object, this project challenges the traditional city scale in a desert master development zoned for vehicles. While the density of program was a driving factor for this approach, it was primarily driven by the desire to create a large-scale interior world, detached from the surrounding developments.

As the potential new venue for the Dubai film festival, entertainment sits at the heart of the project. The lively mix of theater, cinemas, restaurants and bars have been organized into an urban canyon that brings people from the street, down into a shaded entertainment district, culminating in an enclosed oasis, completely removed from the context of surrounding developments. This canyon space is filled with opportunities to see and be seen and is configured to also function as a single huge venue with a meandering red carpet processional route.

To signify the development as you enter the city quarter, the sculptural hotel tower, reminiscent of an Oscar statue, was sited directly in view from the main highway. The design of the hotel tower aimed to create a sense of public destination at various levels when viewed from the ground. By inserting public program between the hotel rooms and the core, lobby spaces are creating at various heights, each designed with unique characteristics that correspond to different room types. The tower culminates in a 60 meter truss that launches off the side of the tower into a suspended sky bar. The loop appears as a hole in the tower at the point at which you enter the building at ground level.

Right | Main building

This spread | Entrance area

CLIENT | Private client
YEAR | 2008
SIZE | 434,332m²
STATUS | In progress
IN COLLABORATION WITH |
Brad Pitt

PROJECT | Restaurant design at Bellagio Casino

FIX RESTAURANT
LAS VEGAS | USA

A mysteriously glowing overhead topography guides visitors into the space and announces the restaurant to its surroundings. The ceiling, made of parallel strips of precision-milled Padouk wood, is shaped in undulating waves, the ribbons of wood alternately converging to form smooth surfaces and diverging to reveal the permeability of the ceiling. Lighting, speakers and air diffusers are concealed within the ceiling. The subtle undulations of the ceiling conceal the air-conditioning and part at strategic points to form eye-shaped air diffusors

Top | Exterior view of the restaurant

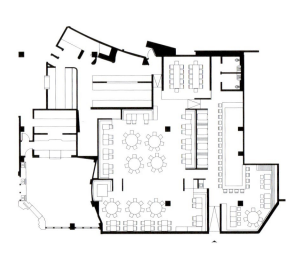

Floor plan

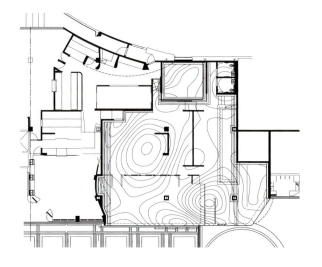

Ceiling plan

CLIENT | LIGHT LV, Andrew Sasson
YEAR | 2003
SIZE | 420m²
STATUS | Built

PROJECT | Urban planning, restaurants, retail

DALIAN AMBER BAY BEACH
DALIAN | CHINA

Amber Bay lies on Binhai Road, Dalian's famous scenic coastal road on the Chinese city's southeast side. Just a fifteen-minute drive from the city center, this picturesque stretch of coastline with its alluring beaches and towering rock formations offers an ideal place for dining and leisure away from noisy downtown Dalian. Within this unique setting, the Amber Bay Beachfront Development provides approximately 10,000m² of restaurants and shopping facilities.

GRAFT's main design intent was to develop an architectural language which complements the natural setting of the sensitive beachfront area.

The design imagined a topographical landscape that could be perceived as a natural configuration of publicly accessible platforms, stairs and roof terraces. The structure's materiality underlines this intention, reflecting the natural palette of the surroundings through its use of bleached wood and surface-treated concrete made of local aggregates.

A boardwalk serves as a public promenade along the half-moon of the beach, its wooden decking providing a natural transition between building and bay, softening the arced edge of the development as it blends into the sand.

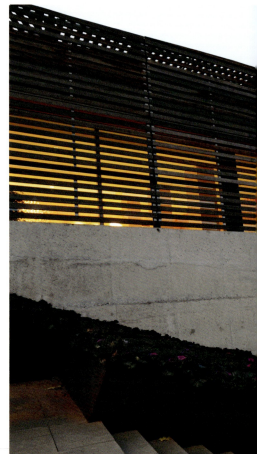

CLIENT | Dalian Amber Bay Development Co. Ltd.
YEAR | 2007
SIZE | 16,000m²
STATUS | Built

PROJECT | Restaurant design

GINGKO BACCHUS
CHENGDU | CHINA

Located in Chengdu, the capital of Sichuan Province in China, the Gingko Bacchus Restaurant is a surrealistic blend (a "graft") of Western and Chinese restaurant and food culture.

The starting point for the design is a blacked out space. The public spaces are considered a river or a stream along which one "floats" through the depth of the 1,200m² black space. The stream begins at the elevators, the public entrance to the restaurant on the fourth floor of the Gingko Restaurant Building. The wavy wood ribbon ceiling and stainless steel intarsia of the floor pattern evoke a sense of flow along the "stream" which leads to an open dining and show cooking area. Eight private dining rooms are located like boulders along the stream, each color-coded and themed by food and famous Bacchus depictions.

Food is used in various layers of abstraction throughout the restaurant. Each private dining room has its own custom wallpaper of simple food produce – carrots, mushrooms, walnuts, broccoli, beans, chilies, or artichokes – made of mirrored and repeated high-resolution images of these vegetables. The color of each room echoes that of its designated vegetable, and together the eight rooms transition gently from green to red.

....

Left | Ceiling detail

Left | Images behind one-way mirrors appear and fade away with a time controlled light system

....

The walls of the stream feature wall-height photographic reinterpretations of traditional Dutch still life paintings. These images are placed behind one-way mirrors equipped with time-controlled back-lighting that makes it possible to highlight or fade out certain aspects of the images. The entire hallway changes in slow motion, the light fading gradually causing the image to disappear and the beholder to appear reflected in the mirror. Like Alice in Wonderland, one finds oneself immersed in a surrealist landscape of giant-sized food. The still life paintings of the Dutch masters make reference to luxury, vanity and cupidity, adding a second layer of meaning through the glorification of the vegetables.

Bacchus (or Dionysus) from antique mythology elevates food to the realm of cult. As the god of wine, earthly delights and their enjoyment, he watches over the guests as they dine exquisite food and wine in the restaurant. Each of the nine rooms features a famous painting of Bacchus – for example, Caravaggio's depiction of Bacchus as a young "Boy with a Fruit Basket", or the "Triumph of Bacchus" by Velázquez – but in an abstracted, pixelated representation laser-cut out of sheet stainless steel. The illuminated background of the vegetable wallpapers and Arcadian landscapes can be seen through the laser-cut pixels of the historical Bacchus paintings.

The ceiling of the dining rooms reverses the play of foreground and background: here images of nymphs – the playmates of Bacchus – can be glimpsed from certain angles through pixelated and laser-cut images of grapes. This sexual undertone is repeated in the custom-designed counters, tables and sofas, which are composed of two elements in different forms of embrace, fusion and separation.

Dark-tinted mirrors and reflective surfaces are used throughout the restaurant to create surrealistic extensions of space, blurring the guest's orientation. Overhead mirrors make the public dining room appear double the height. TV screens concealed above the one-way mirrors create the impression of frameless images floating between spaces. At various different points, illumination is used to create illusions of space, luring the beholder towards objects that are actually behind surfaces. Illusion and reflection are ever-present aspects of the restaurant design.

But the highlight of the restaurant is the food itself: an intriguing fusion of international cuisine with Chinese influences, enhanced by the famous flavors of the Ginkgo Restaurant Group. GRAFT's work also included the entire graphic design of the restaurant, from the wallpapers to the menus.

Left | Hallway
Right | Themed private dining room

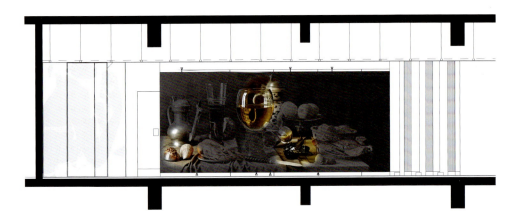

Corridor elevation

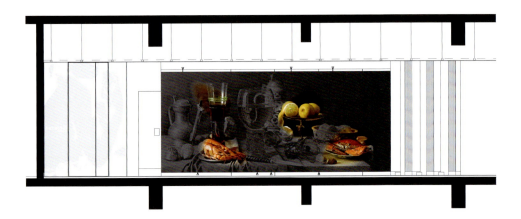

Corridor elevation

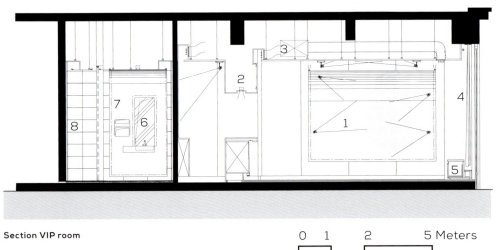

Section VIP room

1. Bacchus themed perforated black painted stainless steel
2. Bird eye mapple black veneer bar counter
3. Air conditioning system in ceiling
4. Colored velvet curtain
5. Bird eye mapple black veneer TV counter
6. Toilet's mirror
7. Black painted steel
8. Toilet's black granite tiles

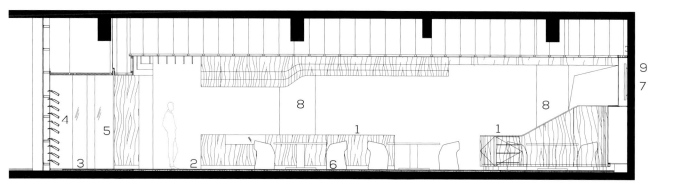

Section public area

1. Bird eye mapple black veneer
2. Black stainless steel
3. Hardwood parquet
4. Wine bottle holder
5. Toughened glass
6. Black granite flooring with stainless steel stip
7. One-way mirror
8. mirror
9. Plasma TV

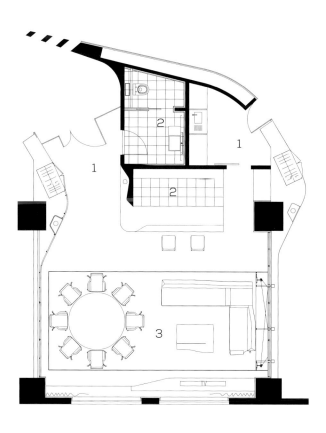

VIP Room

1. Black granite flooring
2. Black granite tile flooring 300x300mm
3. Colored carpet

CLIENT | GINKGO Restaurant Mangement Corporation
YEAR | 2008
SIZE | 1,200m²
STATUS | Built

PROJECT | Restaurant, interior design

BRAND RESTAURANT
LAS VEGAS | USA

The BRAND Steakhouse sits amidst the casino floor in the Monte Carlo Hotel in Las Vegas. The marriage of texture and form coupled with variations in height creates a varied spatial experience. The mesmerizing, shifting pattern of the ceiling panels and the rich, ambient materials – smoked oak flooring, leather and suede upholstery, cowhide, tree branched mirrors and animated LED panels – create an interior that varies with one's standpoint and introduces a palette of natural materials within the hyper-synthetic environment of the casino. The low walls of the restaurant, their arrangement echoing that of the ceiling panels, afford an open view of the restaurant, inviting passers-by in the casino to step in, and evoke associations with the wooden fences of a ranch. The ceiling canopy is the jewel of the space. Comprised of numerous panels wrapped in custom-printed fur, the canopy reveals itself on closer inspection to be an intricately distributed, pixelated abstraction of a cowhide pattern. The layered arrangement of backlit panels creates a spectacular dusty glow that is both mesmerizing and comforting, and both visually intricate but in its overall impression calming. The ceiling rises towards the back of the restaurant, affording a view of the "animated" ceiling from within.

....

The canopy consists of 255 panels in eight different sizes, made of lightweight aluminum honeycomb panels coated with synthetic hide fabric printed with a cowhide pattern derived from a digital drawing. The panels conceal the mechanical, electrical and plumbing installations and concealed rope lights allow each panel to stand out as an individual element.

The different parts of the restaurant – the lounge, main dining area, and private dining areas – are spatially distinct but not totally enclosed. Walkways gently rise and fall into different spaces, orchestrating a gradual promenade through different atmospheric zones. Sliding glass partitions and bronze curtains provide delicate, variable separations between restaurant and casino. Unexpected visual connections tie the spaces together, providing an array of opportunities for voyeurism and social contact.

The separation of ground and ceiling planes is most evident in the lounge area, where the dynamic undulations of the ceiling frame an intimate space for the guests separate from but open to its surroundings. Despite its proximity to the casino, it is a sheltered, more intimate space. Sliding bronzed-glass partitions and sheer panels provide additional separation without interrupting the visual continuity of the space. The bar as the focal point at the far end of the lounge adds a new dimension to BRAND, its black-mirrored backdrop and polished stone counter reflecting the amber glow of the room.

The main dining area is divided into three zones, the floor gradually terracing upwards towards the back of the restaurant, elevating the diners above the casino. Here the diners become part of the spectacle. Various table layouts, carefully orchestrated to heighten the fine dining experience, can accommodate a wide range of groups from a couple to a larger group. The far wall of the dining area is a long bronze-mirrored surface etched with a pattern of glowing pixelated tree branches, allowing guests to subtly observe the reflected space behind while enjoying the abstracted forest.

The private dining area is the most exclusive part of the restaurant with a quite different interior. For maximum privacy, frosted glass sliding partitions can be closed to provide separation within the room itself, as well as from the rest of the restaurant. Subtly shifting light behind the mica wall above a wooden credenza creates the impression of a landscape beyond, reducing the sense of enclosure.

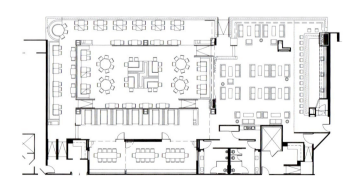

Floor plan

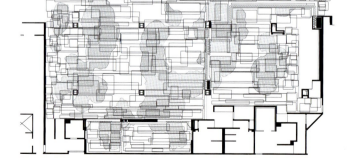

Ceiling plan

CLIENT | MGM Mirage Design Group
YEAR | 2008
SIZE | 700m²
STATUS | Built

PROJECT | Masterplan, ski jump facilities, hotel, residential, restaurant, spa

CHANGBAISHAN SKI JUMPS
WANGTIANE | CHINA

After two decades of infrastructural and urban development, China is now also expanding rapidly in the tourism sector. To promote faster growth, the Chinese government declared several "tourism formation zones". One of these is the area around the spectacular Changbai volcano in the province Jilin, adjoining the border to North Korea. The region is dominated by vast forests that extend as far as Siberia. The permafrost between November and April makes the area a potential tourist mecca for winter sports. GRAFT was asked to design and plan the "Changbai Mountain Slopes". The entire project extends to six million m² at three different locations. In the valley of "Manjiang", GRAFT planned an amusement park, show theater, exhibition space, thermal baths that exploit the natural hot fountains, a village with numerous boutiques, restaurants and cafés as well as 3,000 guest rooms in hotels and mansions. "Hengsahn" is an area of rolling hills where a larger village and several resort hotels are planned, with special focus on preventive medicine and cultural lifestyles. And finally, in "Wangtiane", a skiing region is being planned that will be the largest of its kind in Asia.

....

Left top | View onto ski jump area and train station
Left bottom | Train station
Right | Adjacent village with retail and hospitality facilities

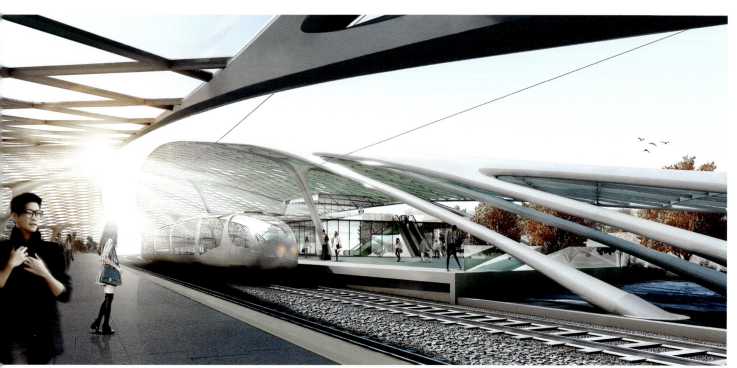

The regional design plan envisages a series of locations with distinct, individual architectural characters that complement one another. A new train station connects the different business and entertainment locations, networking the locations with a hi-speed link. A total of three ski jumps are planned – two of Olympic dimensions, and a third flying hill for extremely long jumps – and will be the future emblem of Wangtiane. The entire complex is conceived as multi-functional facility incorporating restaurants, VIP lounges and hotels. Construction of the preparatory infrastructure will start in 2016, and the project will proceed in multiple phases from 2016 to 2020.

This spread | Public spaces and shopping area

CLIENT | Zhonghong Investment Co. Ltd.
YEAR | 2010
SIZE | 6,000,000m²
STATUS | In progress

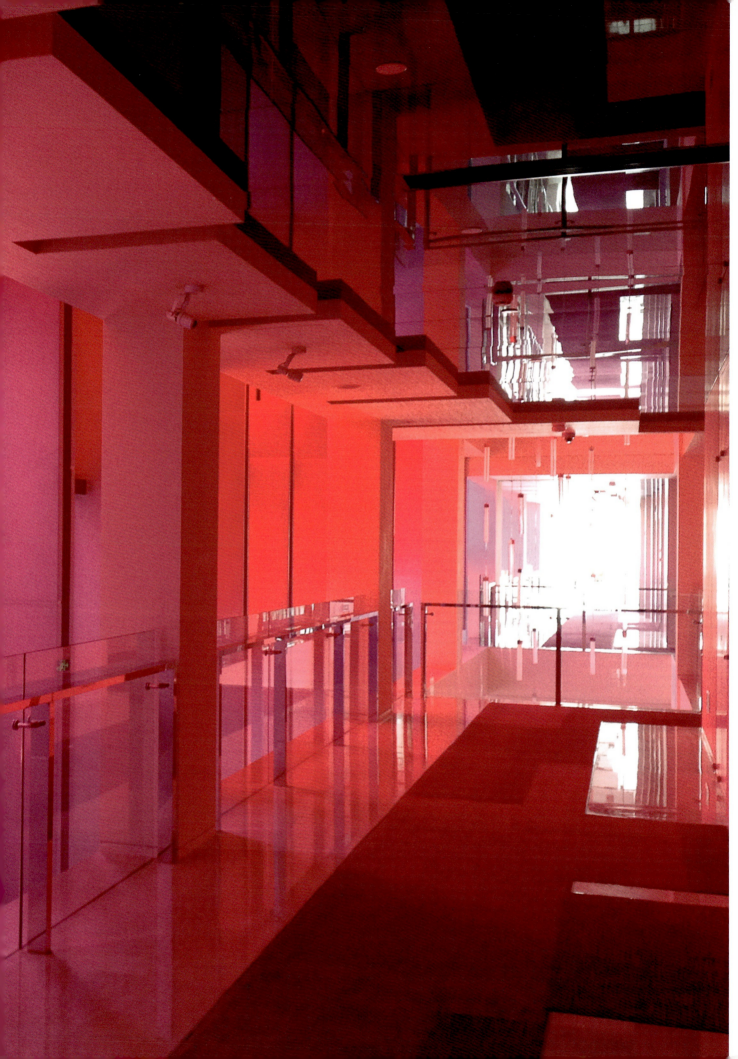

PROJECT | Hotel, restaurant, interior and façade design

GALLERY HOTEL
BEIJING | CHINA

Next to the Workers' Stadium, right in the center of Beijing's night life area, GRAFT designed a sixty-room boutique hotel. Although the original design of the building is by the Chinese architect Wang Hui, GRAFT was commissioned to extend and complete it including the landscape design, the eastern façade, extensions of the ground floor area, and all of the public zones of the interior. The guest rooms were designed by six different designers, with GRAFT responsible for five rooms including the presidential suite.

The design follows the principle of a shifted grid. The original architecture of Wang Hui is based on shifting cubes, each housing a hotel room. GRAFT adopted this system, divided it further into smaller units, and added a dynamic distortion following underlying spline-based geometries. The splines run perpendicular to the grid and create a sculptural movement along the length of the building, which manifests itself both in the interior and exterior.

GRAFT's design for the eastern façade starts at the north end as a traditional curtain wall, slowly peeling off the building along the façade until it becomes an independent structure. This sculptural movement forms the main entrance and a twenty-meter-high void for the café and restaurant. The hotel corridor will be flooded with morning light through the purple glass of the façade, showering the hotel guests with a sensation of color upon opening their room doors in the morning. At night the purple glass construction is visible through the Papula trees lining the street, creating a unique destination.

Left | Façade from the inside

Left | Guest room
Right | Restaurant

CLIENT | China Modern Art Hotel Management Co., Ltd.
YEAR | 2009
SIZE | 8,000m²
STATUS | Built

PROJECT | Masterplanning, tourism development

MYSTERY BAY
HAINAN | CHINA

Mystery Bay to the south of the Lingshui Bay development offers a special combination of qualities that make it an ideal place for a hotel resort. In addition to its pristine beaches, the resort's secluded bay, enclosed naturally by a steep mountain ridge to the northeast and steep cliffs at either end, gives it an advantage over other beaches in Hainan. Privacy and seclusion is guaranteed.

But unlike many resorts where this kind of privacy is offset by a long distance to any entertainment of cultural features, Mystery Bay is a five-minute drive from a golf club and a ten-minute drive from the Lingshui Bay new town development with its high-rise CBD, galleries in the canal town, convention centers, theme parks and entertainment facilities.
The design of the resort hotel responds to this setting with a cinematographic strategy which through its storyboard emphasizes and enhances the special quality of the location. Guests arriving from the bustling development of

Lingshui leave the high-rise towers and freeway and drive through smaller settlements, before passing by a golf course set in a beautiful landscape and up a narrow valley into Bai Nui Mountain where they arrive at a tunnel. Emerging into bright sunlight at the other end of the tunnel, they see the sea and a large lake, its far end blurring into the sky like an infinity pool. Letters spelling the name of the hotel appear to float on the reflective surface.

The road appears to lead on into the lake, its destination unclear, before spiralling down mysteriously beneath the water's surface to a place beneath the lake, where the temperature is cooler and the blinding light gives way to an intricate play of shadows and bright spots, where the sun shines through windows in the bottom of the lake. Arriving at the hotel, the guests enjoy a 270-degree panoramic view of the ocean from the reception. After checking in the scene changes: the guest descends into a cool canyon

Right | Hotel sitting on steep mountain ridge

This spread | Resort villas

Left | Beach club and hotel are connected via the "inclinator"
Right | Tropical canyon wall

....

with lush tropical vegetation on the landward side and access to the hotel rooms facing the sea. The temperature is cool, the light comfortably shaded, the air filled with the sounds of tropical birds living in the "canyon". Entering their room, guests at first see greenish, reflected light, but on opening the colored glass shutters are greeted with the same 270-degree view of the bay. As all rooms are accessed from one side only, every room has this spectacular view.

Once settled in, guests can explore the resort. The cool, cave-like pool and spa is built into the mountainside and is accessible via a passage in the tropical canyon wall. The beach club, on the other hand, is reached via an "inclinator", a diagonally moving elevator car on a track that descends the steep mountain side connecting the hotel and beach. Restaurants, bars and pools are arranged beneath the shade of palm trees, and the existing natural boulders along the beach are used to create an intricate play of terraces. Alternatively, guests can take a winding hiking path from the hotel to the beach bar, passing by a botanical garden and terrarium with local fauna and flora. The cocktail bar at the beach is a special highlight with a swimming pool as its roof. Visitors can relax and enjoy a cocktail while watching swimmers pass overhead as if watching from the seabed.

The oasis is a short walk from the beach club and makes use of a large, flat portion of land at the south end of the bay. Each oasis suite is a single pavilion. Two different typologies of pavilions respond to the topography: beach-front pavilions that look like futuristic vessels hovering above the beach and vegetation, ready to depart back into the sea at a moment's notice; and hillside pavilions clustered as cabana-like buildings on terraces in the topography, gradually ascending the hillside.

Further up the mountain side above the hotel are the resort villas. Each is between 1,200m² and 2,500m² in size and nestled in amongst the steep terrain.

———

Left top | Beach club
Left bottom | Beach club swim bar
Right | Resort villas above the hotel

Left | Sunset bar interior
Right | Sunset bar

CLIENT | Chengdu Wide Horizon Investment Group Co., Ltd.
YEAR | 2013
SIZE | 55,800m²
STATUS | In progress

PROJECT | Hotel resort

W HOTEL AND RESORT
PALM SPRINGS | USA

GRAFT was invited to develop a luxury hotel resort on the outskirts of Palm Springs, California. Surrounded by a manmade landscape of green golf courses, the project reinstates a desert landscape to the site, linking it to its cosmological context by utilizing wind circulation and celestial events. A series of canyons cut into the landscape produce shade and privacy for guests on their way to their hotel suites. Designed in dune-shaped forms, the orientation of these canyons responds to the mountain views and the local wind and climate conditions. The architecture is married to the landscape, generating a topographically spatial and unique storyboard. There are three distinct canyons that generate different atmospheres and experiences throughout the hotel. The water canyon creates a space for an expansive pool area in the form of a flooded landscape, featuring the main restaurant. Facing west, the water canyon will cool down the hotel considerably as daily winds rush over the body of water that reflects the brilliant colors of sunset at the end of each day.

The tree canyon offers shadow and freshness under a canopy of indigenous sycamore trees. Here, guests will find amenities such as a grotto spa and a green open-air theater, experiencing the seasons as the leaves change colors in the fall.

....

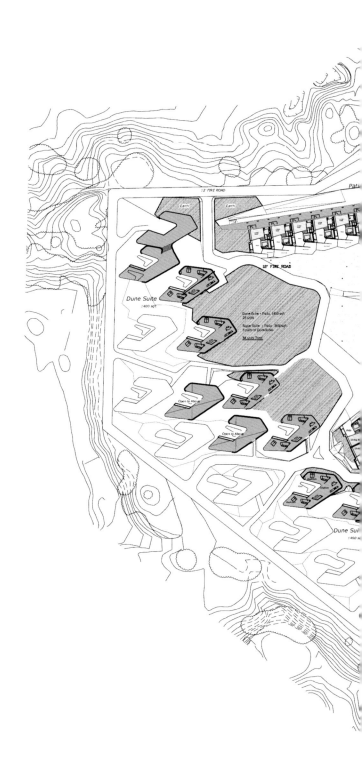

Site plan

Right | Pool bar
Left | Crater restaurant

The sand canyon features the Crater restaurant, defined by dining on water, surrounded by walls of fire, outside under the stars. The canyon leads guests to hotel suites shaped in a "dunescape" that are open to the wind, sunsets and mountain views, yet provide complete privacy.

The project uses landscape to produce an exclusive oasis within an increasingly overdeveloped desert. In balance with nature, it employs indigenous arid plantation and the organic powers of sun, wind and site-specific conditions to conserve energy and natural resources. As a result, the desert hotel will need air conditioning only 20% of the year.

CLIENT | Starwood Hotels and Resorts Worldwide, Inc.
YEAR | 2005
SIZE | 18,000m²
STATUS | In progress

PROJECT | Restaurant design

WOK-A-LICIOUS
BERLIN | GERMANY

Wokalicious – from "wok" and "delicious" – is Thai fusion cuisine from finest ingredients. Situated in the heart of Berlin Mitte in the just accomplished "Hackesches Quartier", the spatial concept reflects the character of the menu: light, organic and natural, in a balance of diversity and clarity.

While open to square and street with ample shop windows, the restaurant's back wall is carried out as a horizontally structured wooden relief, which in materiality, curvature and stacking reminds of the characteristic bamboo baskets in which the delicious dim sums are prepared and served. Swinging from the entrance along the whole length of the restaurant, the relief connects its three main parts: The main dining area (dining) in the western part, the central bar with a double counter and open show kitchen (short stay) and the lounge-like "private dining" in the back part (relaxing) with seating bench and lounge chairs. The lounge can be divided off by a curtain and used separately by groups in a flexible way.

Reflective film on the narrow sides of the wooden relief results in brightly illuminating reflexes according to the standpoint of the beholder and the exposure to light – subtle zest in the predominantly mild and natural mix of materials. Apart from soft indirect lighting, the protruding light object Ameba focuses on the central gallery of tables in the main dining area.

Natural materials in the dining area, and dark almost black materials in the lavatories, form a strong contrast to accentuating gold of glass mosaic tiles, wallpapers and painted surfaces.

CLIENT | Private client
YEAR | 2011
SIZE | 320m²
STATUS | Built

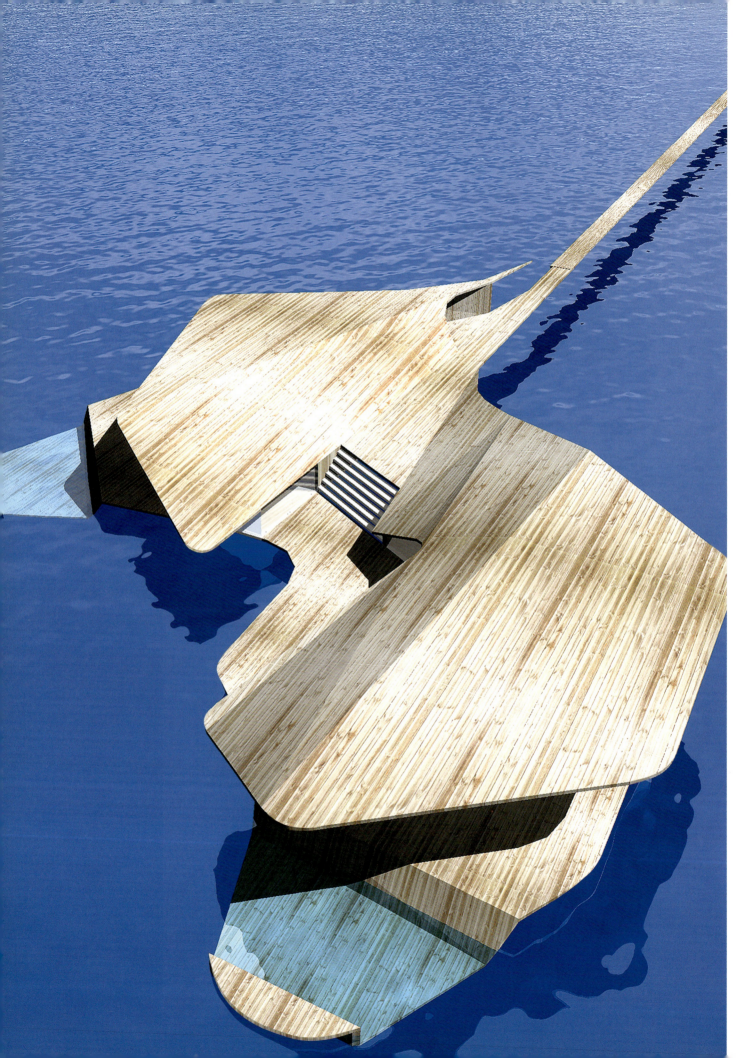

PROJECT | Hotel and resort design

WATER CAY LUXURY HOTEL RESORT
TURKS AND CAICOS ISLANDS

GRAFT was asked to develop a design and storyboard for a high-end luxury resort on a Caribbean island in Turks and Caicos.

The hotel concept envisages three sets of room types and experiences, located near to a central point at the north-west tip of the island, next to Half Moon Bay. All three experiences are reachable from this public center and, like pearls on a string, form three lines that echo characteristic features of the island. Each has a strong and distinctive atmosphere derived from their setting: on water, in the trees, at the cliff edge. The design for each room and structure responds to its specific location and condition, enhancing its quality and providing a unique experience.

This spread | Site plan

This spread | Cliff villas

CLIFF VILLAS

Cliff villas on the beautiful north-western cliff expose vistas toward stunning beaches and crystal Caribbean waters. The villa compound consists of three volumes that are separate but geometrically related, as if cut out of a single prismatic block. Formed from limestone, corals, alabaster, driftwood and linen sails, they create a small village situation. The pool and outside areas are integrated into the topography, taking advantage of the natural setting and different heights. Fully-equipped cabanas are carved like caves into the cliff with private decks cascading down to the beach, making inhabitable the threshold between land and water.

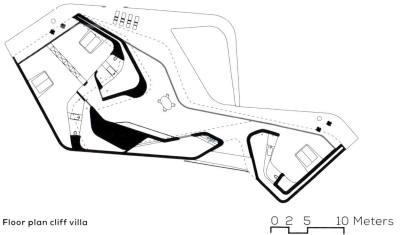
Floor plan cliff villa

0 2 5 10 Meters

This spread | Water pavilions

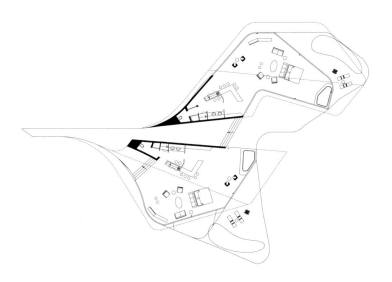

Floor plan water pavilion

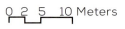

WATER PAVILIONS

Water pavilions float in the bay like seabirds ready for take-off and offer panoramic views of the sunrise and sunset. The units have two rooms, accessed via a shared entrance and walkway, that can be rented independently or together. At high tide, the water leaves only islands of wooden deck "floating" in front of the units. At low tide, a connecting walkway is exposed, that leads to so-called "tidal pools" that retain water from the sea as it departs. These suites offer an amphibious and direct experience of the tidal phenomenon.

This spread | Tree houses

TREE HOUSES

Located on a high inland ridge, the tree houses are placed at specific high points, nestled in and above the foliage, four to five meters above ground. These arboreal units offer views of the northern and southern shores, the inner bay and the western seaboard. Arranged in clusters of three, they appear to hover in the trees like blossoms opening to the sun. Two to three clusters of tree houses share a common pool and barbeque area at elevated platforms, from which gently ramping walkways lead up to the individual units. By exploiting the topography, steep inclines and steps should be minimized.

CLIENT | Starwood Capital
YEAR | 2006
SIZE | 18,000m²
STATUS | In progress

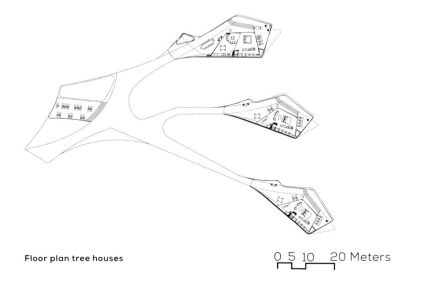

Floor plan tree houses

0 5 10   20 Meters

PROJECT | Hotel, tourism development

BONDS CAY ISLAND RETREAT
BAHAMAS

Bonds Cay is an uninhabited island in the Bahamas with lush vegetation and long stretches of beach and ironshore coastline. The firms GRAFT, Gardiner&Theobald, james corner field operations, BuroHappold and ATM were commissioned to create a masterplan guided by the principles of nature and the potential of the island.
To ensure the design would fully respect the natural environment, several field trips were undertaken to study weather conditions, identify buildable areas and understand the rich ecology of the island. The east of the 600-acre island of Bonds Cay is exposed to the ocean while the Great Bahama Bank extends to the west for about 25 miles. The value of the island's wildlife is a product of the diverse mosaic of ecologies. The ambitious masterplan had to comply with rigorous, sustainable guidelines and attempts to bring people to the island to enjoy its diverse beauty without negatively impacting on it. The building plan therefore excludes all areas susceptible to erosion or storm surge flooding and of high ecological value, and focuses on a zone of development that would have least impact on the island. The center of the island is a nature reserve with no villas and only a spa and water sports center on the central lagoon.

....

Right | Bird's view of the island

Concentrating buildings within the development zone as much as privacy allows, retains as much unbroken ecologies on the island as possible. By lifting the buildings off the ground where possible, the physical footprint of the development is reduced. The masterplan foresees areas where ecologies could be enriched beyond what they are today with the aim of achieving a net zero loss of ecology.

NORTH ISLAND VILLAGE

A further aim of the Bonds Cay development is to positively impact the socioeconomic situation of the Berry Islands and the Bahamas as a whole. The village serves as a centerpiece, encouraging a diverse mix of residents, hotel guests, island staff and artists in residence. Strategically sited in the most sheltered part of the island, it wraps around a lagoon marina and comprises four principle public areas: a community center, an elevated plaza, a market place and a village beach. The integrated approach to the island infrastructure and back of house program means the village will be a functional combination of residential, commercial, civil and infrastructural buildings.

THE BOUTIQUE HOTEL

Guests arrive at the hotel by sea plane where there is a single restaurant and bar on the beach at the southern peninsula of the island. An elevated boardwalk leads through a mangrove full of wildlife to the reception area and onto one of 30 individual suites nestled into the foliage, each with its own sunset view, sea access and pool. Each area and suite has a different character to create as rich a variety of experiences as possible. The hotel should give people access to the natural beauty of the area in the least invasive way.
Pathways lead guests and residents through every area of interest on the island, including an observatory, art gallery and institute for sustainability. The masterplan for Bonds Cay is a fusion of nature, art and science.

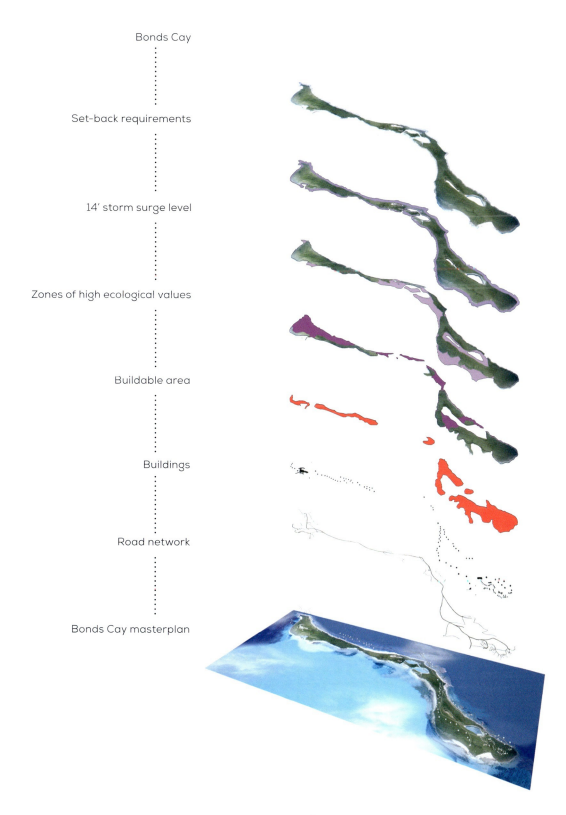

Right | Establishing buildable area

Boutique hotel

Community residences

Community residences

Rock reef loop 2.7km

Wellness cen[ter]

Watersport and diving center

Lagoon loop 4.6km

This spread | Communal area from above

CLIENT | Confidential
SIZE | 2,600,000m²
YEAR | 2009
STATUS | In progress

HOSPITALITY PROJECTS
WORLDWIDE

HOTEL DOMINION
FONTANA
VIVA BAR

FIX RESTAURANT >> p.412
HOTEL Q! BERLIN >> p.364
W HOTEL AND RESORT >> p.468

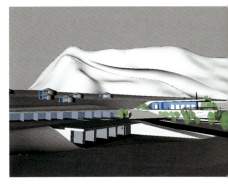

WATER CAY LUXURY HOTEL RESORT >> p.480
SAMANA LUXURY RESORT >> p.396
DALIAN AMBER BAY >> p.418
HOTEL MONGOLIA

TEXTIL
D RESTAURANT >> p.436
RT CANYON RESORT >> p.406
RESTAURANT & BAR >> p.400

HOTEL IVERIA >> p.330
THE EMPEROR BEIJING >> p.384
GINGKO BACCHUS >> p.424

SIX SENSES NANXUN
SICHUAN AIR T3 LOUNGE
CITY CENTER'S ARIA POOL DECK >> p.356
CITY CENTER'S ARIA RESTAURANT AND BAR

HOSPITALITY PROJECTS
WORLDWIDE

HOTEL CHENGDU
VERTICAL VILLAGE >> p.350
CHANGBAISHAN SKI JUMP >> p.442

W HOTEL NEW YORK >> p.344
GALLERY HOTEL >> p.452
BONDS CAY ISLAND RETREAT >> p.492

SPRING RESORT BEIJING
PEACOCK
ITALIAN VILLAGE TIANJIN BOUTIQUE HOTEL
WOK-A-LICIOUS >> p.474

HAUS DOLDER
AN HOTSPRING RESORT
L LOFER >> p.374
ATLAS

HOTEL BOSTALSEE >> p.308
YOUTH HOSTEL MUNICH >> p.322
BRLO BRWHOUSE >> p.316

MYSTERY BAY >> p.458
HOTEL GAMMARTH >> p.288
OLD MILL HOTEL >> p.276
FAMILY HOUSE SANKT AUGUSTIN >> p.300

GRAFT WORLD

BEIJING | CHINA

| GERMANY
SHOOP | GERMANY

INN | ESTONIA
LATVIA
● MOSCOW | RUSSIA
LATVIA

| GERMANY
AW | POLAND
| GERMANY
| GERMANY

DE | SERBIA
TBILISI | GEORGIA ● TSINANDALI | GEORGIA
● BATUMI | GEORGIA
ISTANBUL | TURKEY

● CHANGBAISHAN MOUNTAIN | CHINA
● QIN HUANG DAO | CHINA
● DALIAN | CHINA
TIAN JIN | CHINA
YANTAI | CHINA   ● SEOUL | KOREA   ● TOKYO | JAPAN
● WUHAN | CHINA
● CHENG DU | CHINA

● DUBAI | UNITED ARAB EMIRATES
● MUSCAT | OMAN

HONGKONG | CHINA   ● AODI | TAIWAN
● HAINAN | CHINA

● HO CHI MINH | VIETNAM

● ADDIS ABABA | ETHIOPIA

● KUALA LUMPUR | MALAYSIA

● NAIROBI | KENYA
KIGALI | RUANDA

● DAR ES SALAAM | TANZANIA

GABORONE | BOTSWANA

AUCKLAND | NEW ZEALAND ●

MAHANA | NEW ZEALAND ●

ABOUT GRAFT

Lars Krückeberg, Wolfram Putz and Thomas Willemeit founded GRAFT in 1998 in Los Angeles, California, as a studio for architecture, urban planning, design, music and "the pursuit of happiness". With a team of more than 100 creatives and further offices in Berlin and Beijing, GRAFT has designed and managed a wide range of projects in multiple disciplines and locations.

While the office's core activities center on the field of architecture and the built environment, GRAFT has always maintained an interest in crossing boundaries between disciplines and "grafting" the creative potential and methodologies of different realms. The studio therefore also works in the fields of exhibition design, product design, art installations and academic projects. Lars Krückeberg Wolfram Putz and Thomas Willemeit have held several guest professorships in the US and in Germany and are members of the expert team of the German research institute Zukunftsinstitut.

In 2014, GRAFT's partners founded GRAFT Brandlab together with branding expert Linda Stannieder in order to additionally focus on communication design, brand strategy and consultancy while staying true to GRAFT's multi-disciplinary approach and working methods.

In 2007, Brad Pitt started the "Make It Right Foundation" together with GRAFT, Bill McDonough and the Cherokee Foundation, to rebuild the Lower 9th Ward in New Orleans after Hurricane Katrina.

GRAFT's self-initiated projects also include the SOLARKIOSK AG founded together with the German lawyer Andreas Spiess in 2009 to bring clean energy, connectivity and solar products to rural areas in sub-Saharan Africa. And in 2015, GRAFT co-founded Heimat2 with H.W. Pausch (Synergy Productions), Sven Rawe (Bernstein Group) and Dr. Gert Ellinghaus (Comterra Development Group), which aims to bring dignified housing solutions to refugees in Europe.
Lars Krückeberg, Wolfram Putz and Thomas Willemeit wrote GRAFT HOME. STORY. together with Nora Zerelli, public relations manager at GRAFT since 2012, and PR assistant Yvonne Corinna Paul.

The layout and cover design arose in a collaborative process together with GRAFT's partner firm Brandlab. Achmad Razzaq, Miranda Squire and Tom Hutton were responsible for the layout and typesetting, Yvonne Corinna Paul and Nora Zerelli for the illustration editing.

GRAFTIES

LIST OF CURRENT AND FORMER GRAFT DESIGNERS, ARCHITECTS AND ARTISTS,
THAT GRAFT HAS THE PRIVILEGE OF CALLING CO-WORKERS AND FRIENDS

Aaron Thomsen
Achmad Razzaq
Adwitya Dimas Satria
Agata Glubiak
Agnieszka Wiejak
Ai Honda
Aileen Schüler
Alaa Haddad
Aleca Bunescu
Alejandra Lillo
Alejandro Gonzalez
Aleksandra Kiszkielis
Alexandra Schindl
Aleksandra Zajko
Alessandra Pantuso
Alex Jackson
Alex Liu Cheng
Alexander Grasser
Alexander Jackson
Alexander Jacobs
Alexander Niederhaus
Alexandra Kubos-Nowak
Alexandra Nikolova
Alexandra Tobescu
Alexandra Zajko
Alfredo Peñafiel Suarez
Alice Mayer
Alicia Brown
Alison Winchester
Allison Weiler
Altan Arslanoglu
Alyse Sedlock
Ana Maria Galvez Castillo
Andrea Göldel
Andrea Perle
Andrea Schütte
Andrei-Dan Musetescu
Andy Bryant
Angelika Rehe
Anika Klos
Anita Ackermann
Anita Eyrich
Anja Frenkel
Anja Ludwig
Anna Frey
Anna Lena Kortmann
Anna Pilarska
Anna Wittwer
Annabel Cremer
Anne Prestel
Annette Finke
Annette Kniepkamp
Anthony Ruan Jing
Antoine Mahiou
Antonio Luque
Arndt Prager

Arne Petersen
Arne Wegner
Arvid Wölfel
Asami Tachikawa
Assaf Ruder
Atsushi Sugiuchi
Aurelius Weber
AnnikaSaenger
Balthasar Vogel
Barbara Caesar
Benjamin Ennemoser
Benjamin Rieß
Bernd Wölfel
Bernhard Dal-Bianco
Berta Sola
Bertil Donker
Bika Rebek
Björn Rolle
Blaz Solar
Brandon Love
Brian Nelson
Brian Wickersham
Bryan Flaig
Burk Greenwood
Carla Gertz
Carola Morczinneck
Carsten Dankert
Carsten Gauert
Casey McSweeney
Casey Rehm
Celi Freeman
Chelsea Chan Hei
Chris Li Ju
Christian Litz
Christian Precht
Christian Taeubert
Christina Cho
Christina Gmeindl
Christine Huber
Christoph Jantos
Christoph Körner
Christoph Rauhut
Christopher Nielsen
Chung-Yang Cheng
Claudia Bayer
Claudia Kessner
Claudia Tong
Clemens Hochreiter
Constanze Elges
Constanze Stark
Cornelia Faisst
Cristina Freni
Crystal Tang
Dagmar Niecke
Dalma Vitez
Dana Bauer

Daniel Büning
Daniel Finck
Daniel Krüger
David Schwarz
David Tyl
Denis Hegic
Dennes Janßen
Dennis Hawner
Dennis Pohl
Dieter Walk
Dietmar Koering
Dietmar Köring
Dirk Pause
Djordje Zdravkovic
Dongmin Shin
Donna Riedel
Doreen Rehmer
Dorian Bybee
Dorothea von Rotberg
Duo Ning
Eddie Hermann
Edward Hermann
Elena Suarez
Elizabeth Pritchett
Elizabeth Wendell
Emma Rytoft
Eric Spencer
Eun-hae Kwon
Evangelos Pantazis
Evgenia Dimopoulou
Falko Landenberger
Fei Liang
Felipe Wagner
Felix Götze
Felix Grauer
Filipa Leal de Carvalho
Firat Ertegi
Florencia Carvajal
Florian Niedworok
Francesca Rose
Frank Lin
Frank Petters
Franzi Fischer
Frederieke Reich
Gasper Arh
Genevieve Lim
Georg Schmidthals
Georgina Huljich
Gerfried Hinteregger
Gerrit Hoppe
Gilbert Wigankow
Greg Ramirez
Gregor Hoheisel
Gu Yan
Guenter Buschta
Gunhild Niggemeier

Gunnar Krempin
Han Xu
Hans-Georg Bauer
Helena Westerlind
Helena Willemeit
Hendrik Lindemann
Henning Fritsch
Henning Götz
Henning Ströh
Hiro Yamamoto
Hotao Chow
Howard Wang
Ian-Stefan Chis
Ilias Klis
Ines Bergdoldt
Ing Tse Chen
Inga Anger
Inigo de Latorre
Ioanna Piniara
Irina Kostka
Irmgardt Reiter
Isak Birgersson
Iulian Ivan
Ivan Soldo
Izabela Pavel
Jakub Wreczycki
James Backwell
James Lowder
Jamie Norden
Jan Saggau
Jan-Philipp Herms
Jana Deters-Gonseth
Jana Fröbel
Janghee Yoo
Janka Lengyel
Jannis Jaschke
Jannis Merz
Jasper Borg
Javier Nieto Cano
Jean-Rémi Houel
Jeannine Pauer
Jeffrey Kim
Jennifer Scarlett Khan
Jens Hecht
Jens Mehlan
Jeremy Fletcher
Jerzy Gabriel
Jia Chen
Jian Lu Bi
Jiang Yi
Joanna Zielinska
Johan Tali
Johanna Kuntze
Johannes Staudt
Johannes Staudt
John Michael Haas

508

John Hearne
John Shen
Jonas Aarsoe-Larsen
Jonas Droste
Jonathan Oelschlig
Jörg Dengler
Jürg Stanzel
Joshua Gilpin
Julia Borchers
Julia Kliemank
Julia Richter
Julian Busch
Julian Antonius Reiner
Julian Schultz
Julie Hoffmann
Justyna Mintus
Juyen Lee
Kaha Markozashvili
Karla Mueller
Karsten Sell
Kathrin Starcke
Katja Bläsi
Katja Hensel
Katja Mitte
Katja Mydlach
Keizo Okamoto
Kenneth Cameron
Kerry Xie
Kim Harder
Kirsten Klingbeil
Kleopatra Alagialoglou
Konstantin Buhr
Kris Conner
Krista Flascha
Kudzai Magoche
Kurt Bornor
Kurt Hermann
Lan Ream
Lars Krückeberg
Lars Radziejewski
Laura Grüber
Laura Freiling
Laura Knipp
Lennart Wiechell
Leo Clemens
Leo Kocan
Leo Yang
Li Dan Lu
Li Mei
Li Ning
Li Sun Ming
Lidia Beltran Carlos
Liko Zhang Jing
Lilian Yang
Lily Hui Huang
Lin Yu Ju
Linda Stannieder
Liu Qian
Liu Qing
Liu Yixin
Lmke Meissner
Lola Rieger
Lorena Yamamoto
Louis Lefebvre
Luis Berríos Negrón
Lyla Wu
Maik Seidel
Maike Wienmeier
Malgorzata Cvetinovic
Malte Schröder
Marc Antonio Friedhoff Calvo
Marc Schmit
Marcel Kages
Marcus Friesl
Maria Angeles Orduna
Marion Waid
Mark Johnson

Markus Fix
Markus Lager
Markus Müller
Markus Nagler
Markus Wilmers
Marlene Kuelz
Marta Piaseczynska
Martin Franck
Martin Neander
Marvin Bratke
Mary Aramian
Mathilde Catros
Mats Karl Koppe
Matthäus Wasshuber
Matthias Eckardt
Matthias Feulner
Matthias Rümmele
Max Schwitalla
Max Unterfrauner
Max Winchester
Max Wittkopp
Mei Xiao Feng
Melanie Evers
Melanie Schneider
Michael Ahlers
Michael Brown
Michael Cornelsen
Michael Grün
Michael Hirschbichler
Michael Kraus
Michael Mlynek
Michael Zach
Michele Stramezzi
Mick van Gemert
Miloslav Cvetkovic
Mimi Lepis-Levy
Min Zhang
Minh-Luc Pham
Miranda Squire
Mirko Wanders
Maxi Cook
Monika Berstis
Moritz Greiling
Mosska Adeil
Muaaz Odah Bashi
Nadia Kloster
Nam Ji Won
Naoko Miyano
Narineh Mirzaeian
Natalja Kopycko
Nathalie Dziobek Bepler
Nathaphon Phantounarakul
Nathan Miller
Neiel Norheim
Nick Mantis
Nico Bornmann
Nicolas Hugentobler
Nikolas Krause
Nikolay Ivanov
Nils von Minckwitz
Nora Gordon
Nora Zerelli
Nuno Mac
Olaf Dittmers
Oliver André Claußen
Oliver O. Rednitz
Omer Iscimenler
Pam Schriever
Pamela Schriever
Patricia Schneider
Patrick McHugh
Patrik Sonntag
Patryk Pauer
Paul Mandler
Paul Michael Cattaneo
Paula Martin Aedo
Paula Rosch
Paulo De Araujo

Peter Matthew
Peter Tycho-Axelsen
Petra Elm
Pham Minh-Luc
Phil Trigas
Philip Weibhauser
Philipp Ohnesorge
Philipp Utermöhl
Philippe Grotenrath
Phillip Hornung
Phillipe Grothenrath
Phyllis Wang
Pia Panaphet
Pnina Jalon
Primoz Strazar
Priscille Biolley
Puja Shafaroudi
Qi Xiao Wie
Qiu Shi
Ralf Bliem
Ralph Mueller
Raphael Hemmer
Rasa Urnieziute
Rebekka M'Baidanoum
Relana Hense
René Lotz
Ricardo Isaac Valencia Paéz
Richard Ceccanti
Rita Schmidt
Rob DeCosmo
Rus Carnicero
Ruth Kerber
Ruxandra Osiac
Sam You Shao Yong
Sandra Ibarra
Sara Alidadi
Sara Bernardi
Sara Gómez Elorriaga
Sarah John
Sascha Krückeberg
Scott Curie
Sean Guy
Sebastian Filla
Sebastian Gernhardt
Sebastian Lupea
Sebastian Massmann
Sebastian Nastke
Sebastian Sährig
Sebastian Scherer
Sebastian Seyfahrt
Serena Lee
Severin Küppers
Seyavash Zohoori
Shawn Mc Duffee
Shelly Shelly
Sigi Baumgartner
Simon Broll
Simon Takasaki
Simone Gemein
Sonja Wedemeyer
Sophie Ebert
Stefan Beese
Stefan Grohne
Stefan Neudecker
Stefan Ritter
Stefanie Götz
Steffen Ell
Stephan Steeb
Stephan Wiemer
Stephen Form
Stephen Molloy
Steve Simmons
Steven Beites
Suhee Oh
Sun Da Yong
Sunny Wang Xin
Susanne Augustin
Susanne Woitke

Sven Bauer
Sven Fuchs
Sven Neumann
Sven Wesuls
Sybille Paulsen
Sylvain Rocher
Sylvia Stoll
Tade Godbersen
Tamara Pallasch
Tang Fei
Tarak Metha
Taras Breker
Terumoto Mizushima
Thomas Grabner
Thomas Klein
Thomas Neumann
Thomas Niederberger
Thomas Quisinsky
Thomas Rings
Thomas Spindelberger
Thomas Willemeit
Thomas Zeissig
Thorsten Moschüring
Till Mache
Tim Berger
Tim Kolbe
Tim Lange
Tim Sola
Tim Zamora
Timothy Sola
Tin-Shun But
Tina Troester
Tito Walk
Tobias Hein
Tobias Krauth
Tobias Pieper
Tobias Puhlmann
Tom Baecher
Tom Hutton
Tom Mudra
Tony Wei Xin
Tudor Vlasceanu
Ulrich Pohl
Veit Burgbacher
Verena Lihl
Verena Schreppel
Veronica Partelova
Victor Pricop
Victoria Menor-Torres
Vincent Krause
Walter Musacchi
Wang Juan
Wang Yilin
Wilke Mennerich
Wolfgang Grenz
Wolfram Putz
Xavier Osorio
Xiufu Chen
Ye Xiao Dong
Yereem Park
Yo Oshima
Yosi Segas
Yu Fan
Yu-Chieh Chuang
Yuan Yi Fei
Yuki Chen Kun
Yuna Yagi
Yvonne Corinna Paul
Zara Gray
Zhang Ming
Zhang Zhi
Zhao Xin Yue
Zhou Jia Chen
Zhou Wei
Zhou Xue
Zlatko Antolovic

ILLUSTRATION CREDITS

ALL IMAGES, DRAWINGS AND DIAGRAMS © GRAFT, EXCEPT FOR

CONTENTS	(from top to bottom and from right to left)
4	Kevin Fuchs | www.kevinfuchs.com, GRAFT, Tobias Hein, GRAFT, GRAFT, Tobias Hein, Ricky Ridecos, Tobias Hein, Public Domain, GRAFT, Tobias Hein, Nils von Minckwitz, Public Domain, Bauwerk Capital, Tobias Hein, Tobias Hein, GRAFT
5	Jan Bitter, GRAFT, © Kevin Scott, GRAFT, Airteam: Thomas Gorski, GRAFT, GRAFT, GRAFT, GRAFT, Tobias Hein, GRAFT, Fang Zhen Ning, GRAFT, Jeff Granbery, Zumtobel, Tobias Hein, ip design, GRAFT
6	Kanera, Studio Hamm, Hiepler Brunier Architekturfotografie, Tobias Hein, GRAFT, Occhio GmbH, Fotograf: Robert Sprang, Airteam, Marc Heinzelmann, Ulf Saupe / Done Studios Berlin, GRAFT, Hiepler Brunier Architekturfotografie, GRAFT, GRAFT, Ricky Ridecos, Hiepler Brunier Architekturfotografie, GRAFT, L2 Studio
7	GRAFT, Ricky Ridecos, GRAFT, Ricky Ridecos, GRAFT, Golf Tattler: Lai Xuzhu, Ricky Ridecos, GRAFT, GRAFT, GRAFT, GRAFT, Tobias Hein, GRAFT, GRAFT

10	Kevin Fuchs | www.kevinfuchs.com
12/13	Kevin Fuchs | www.kevinfuchs.com
14	Kevin Fuchs | www.kevinfuchs.com
15	Kevin Fuchs | www.kevinfuchs.com
16/17	(right, top) Kevin Fuchs | www.kevinfuchs.com
16/17	(center, bottom) Kevin Fuchs | www.kevinfuchs.com
17	(right, bottom) Kevin Fuchs | www.kevinfuchs.com
18	Kevin Fuchs | www.kevinfuchs.com
19	Kevin Fuchs | www.kevinfuchs.com
26	Tobias Hein
28/29	Tobias Hein
30/31	(right, top) Tobias Hein
30/31	(center, bottom) Tobias Hein
31	(right, bottom) Tobias Hein
34/35	Tobias Hein
53	Tobias Hein
54	(top) Tobias Hein
55	Tobias Hein
56/57	(right, top) Tobias Hein
56/57	(center, bottom) Tobias Hein
57	(right, bottom) Tobias Hein
58/59	Tobias Hein
60	Ricky Ridecos
62/62	Ricky Ridecos
63	Ricky Ridecos
64/65	Ricky Ridecos
67	Tobias Hein
68/69	Tobias Hein
70	Tobias Hein
71	Tobias Hein
74/75	Tobias Hein
75	Tobias Hein
76	Public Domain
78/79	Public Domain
86	Tobias Hein
88/89	Tobias Hein
91	Tobias Hein
92/93	Tobias Hein
94/95	Tobias Hein
97	Nils von Minckwitz
109	Bauwerk Capital
110/111	Bauwerk Capital
112/113	Bauwerk Capital
114	Tobias Hein
116	(bottom) Tobias Hein
117	Tobias Hein
118	(top) Tobias Hein
118	(bottom) Tobias Hein
119	Tobias Hein
120/121	Tobias Hein
123	Tobias Hein
124/125	Tobias Hein
126	(top) Tobias Hein
127	Tobias Hein
128	Tobias Hein
128/129	Tobias Hein
137	Jan Bitter
138/139	Jan Bitter
140/141	Jan Bitter
141	Jan Bitter
143	(bottom) Jan Bitter
144/145	(right, top) Jan Bitter
144/145	(center, bottom) Jan Bitter
145	(right, bottom) Jan Bitter
158/159	© Kevin Scott
169	CD Deutsche Eigenheim
170/171	Airteam, Thomas Gorski
180/181	Tobias Hein
200	Tobias Hein
202/203	Tobias Hein
204	Tobias Hein
214	Fang Zhen Ning
217	Fang Zhen Ning
222	Jeff Granbery
224/225	Jeff Granbery
227	Zumtobel
228	Tobias Hein
231	ip design
235	Kanera
236/237	Kanera
239	Studio Hamm
241	Hiepler Brunier Architekturfotografie
242	(left, top) Ricky Ridecos
242	(left, center) Torsten Seidel Fotografie

242	(left, bottom) Jan Bitter	360/361	Ricky Ridecos
242	(center, top) Fang Zhen Ning	362/363	Ricky Ridecos
242	(center between left and right, center center between top and bottom) Jeff Granbery	364	Hiepler Brunier Architekturfotografie
		366/367	Hiepler Brunier Architekturfotografie
243	(left, bottom) Tobias Hein	368/369	(top) Hiepler Brunier Architekturfotografie
243	(center, bottom) Tobias Hein	370	(top) Hiepler Brunier Architekturfotografie
244	(left, bottom) Tobias Hein	370	(bottom) Hiepler Brunier Architekturfotografie
244	(right, top) Tobias Hein	371	Hiepler Brunier Architekturfotografie
245	(left, top) Tobias Hein	372	Hiepler Brunier Architekturfotografie
245	(left, center) Tobias Hein	372/373	Hiepler Brunier Architekturfotografie
245	(center, bottom) Tobias Hein	384	L2 Studio
245	(left, top) Tobias Hein	386/387	L2 Studio
246	(left, top) Airteam, Thomas Gorski	388	(top) L2 Studio
246	(right, center) Tobias Hein	388	(bottom) L2 Studio
247	(left, center) Kevin Fuchs	www.kevinfuchs.com	392/393	LOSH Mr. Mitsutaka Yokota
247	(center between left and right, center center between top and bottom) Bauwerk Capital	393	LOSH Mr. Mitsutaka Yokota
		394/395	L2 Studio
247	(center, bottom) Nils von Minckwitz	400	Ricky Ridecos
248	Tobias Hein	404	Ricky Ridecos
254	Jan Bitter	404/405	Ricky Ridecos
259	(top) Tobias Hein	412	Ricky Ridecos
259	(bottom) Tobias Hein	414/415	Ricky Ridecos
264	Tobias Hein	416/417	(top) Ricky Ridecos
276	Tobias Hein	424	Golf Tattler: Lai Xuzhu
278/279	Tobias Hein	426/427	Golf Tattler: Lai Xuzhu
281	Tobias Hein	428	(top) Oak Taylor Smith
282/283	(top) Tobias Hein	428	(center) Oak Taylor Smith
282	(left, bottom) Tobias Hein	428	(bottom) Oak Taylor Smith
282	(right, bottom) Tobias Hein	430/431	Golf Tattler: Lai Xuzhu
284	(top) Tobias Hein	431	Golf Tattler: Lai Xuzhu
284	(bottom) Tobias Hein	434/435	Golf Tattler: Lai Xuzhu
285	Tobias Hein	437	Ricky Ridecos
286/287	Tobias Hein	438/439	Ricky Ridecos
300	Jan Kraege	440/441	(top) Ricky Ridecos
302/303	Occhio GmbH, Fotograf: Robert Sprang	475	Tobias Hein
304/305	Tobias Hein	476/477	Tobias Hein
305	Tobias Hein	478/479	Tobias Hein
306/307	Tobias Hein	500	(left, top) Ricky Ridecos
310/311	Airteam, Marc Heinzelmann	500	(left, center) Hiepler Brunier Architekturfotografie
312/313	Airteam, Marc Heinzelmann	500	(center, bottom) Hiepler Brunier Architekturfotografie
316	Ulf Saupe / Done Studios Berlin	501	(left, center) Ricky Ridecos
318/319	Ulf Saupe / Done Studios Berlin	501	(left, bottom) Ricky Ridecos
330	Hiepler Brunier Architekturfotografie	501	(center, top) Hiepler Brunier Architekturfotografie
333	Tobias Hein	501	(center between left and right, center center between top and bottom) L2 Studio
334	Hiepler Brunier Architekturfotografie		
335	Tobias Hein	501	(center, bottom) Golf Tattler: Lai Xuzhu
338/339	Tobias Hein	501	(right, center) Ricky Ridecos
340/341	(top) Hiepler Brunier Architekturfotografie	501	(right, bottom) Ricky Ridecos
340	(left, bottom) Hiepler Brunier Architekturfotografie	502	(right, bottom) Tobias Hein
340/341	(center, bottom) Hiepler Brunier Architekturfotografie	503	(center between left and right, center center between top and bottom) Tobias Hein
357	Ricky Ridecos	503	(center, bottom) Occhio GmbH, Fotograf: Robert Sprang
358/359	Ricky Ridecos	503	(left, bottom) Ulf Saupe / Done Studios Berlin

IMPRINT

GRAFT PARTNERS:
Lars Krückeberg
Wolfram Putz
Thomas Willemeit

GRAFT BRANDLAB PARTNERS:
Linda Stannieder
Lars Krückeberg
Wolfram Putz
Thomas Willemeit

Special thanks to Christoph Korner and Gregor Hoheisel for their invaluable contribution to GRAFT

TEXTS BY:
Lars Krückeberg
Wolfram Putz
Thomas Willemeit
Nora Zerelli

LAYOUT, COVER DESIGN AND TYPESETTING:
GRAFT Brandlab:
Jörg Dengler
Achmad Razzaq
Miranda Squire
Tom Hutton
Yvonne Corinna Paul, GRAFT

PROJECT MANAGEMENT GRAFT:
Nora Zerelli | Berlin

PROJECT MANAGEMENT BIRKHÄUSER:
Henriette Mueller-Stahl | Berlin

COPY EDITING:
Julian Reisenberger | Weimar

ILLUSTRATION EDITING:
Yvonne Corinna Paul | Berlin
Nora Zerelli | Berlin

PRODUCTION:
Katja Jaeger | Berlin

Paper: 135g Hello Fat matt, 1.1
Printing: Holzhausen Druck GmbH, Wolkersdorf

Library of Congress Cataloging-in-Publication data
A CIP catalog record for this book has been applied for at the Library of Congress.

Bibliographic information published by the German National Library
The German National Library lists this publication in the Deutsche Nationalbibliografie; detailed bibliographic data are available on the Internet at http://dnb.dnb.de.

This work is subject to copyright. All rights are reserved, whether the whole or part of the material is concerned, specifically the rights of translation, reprinting, re-use of illustrations, recitation, broadcasting, reproduction on microfilms or in other ways, and storage in databases.
For any kind of use, permission of the copyright owner must be obtained.

This publication is also available as an e-book
(ISBN PDF 978-3-0356-1006-2;
ISBN EPUB 978-3-0356-0990-5).

© 2017 Birkhäuser Verlag GmbH, Basel
P.O. Box 44, 4009 Basel, Switzerland
Part of Walter de Gruyter GmbH, Berlin/Boston

Printed on acid-free paper produced from chlorine-free pulp. TCF ∞

Printed in Austria

ISBN 978-3-0356-1162-5

www.birkhauser.com